Frank Dobson

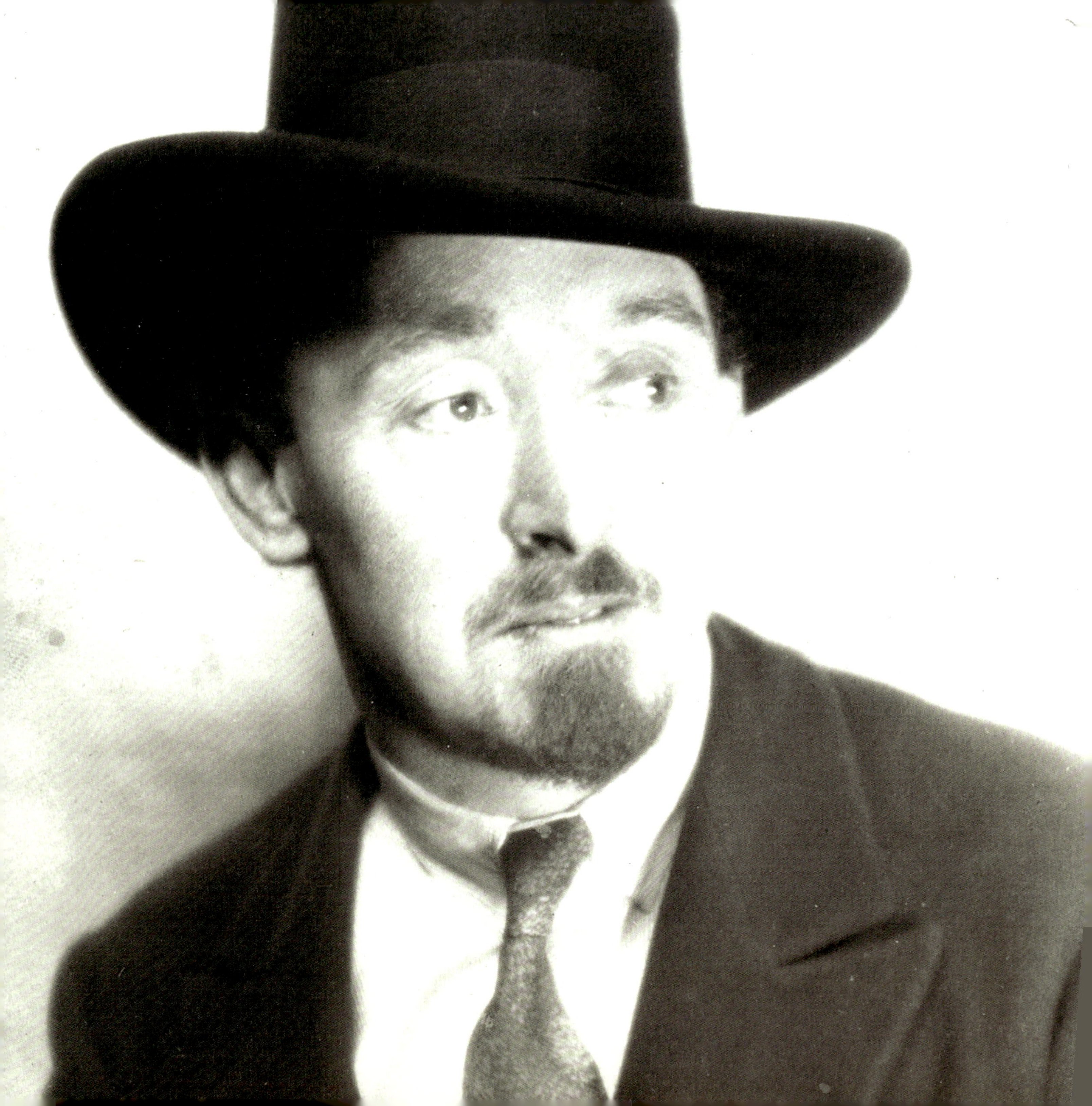

Andrew Lambirth

Frank Dobson

1886-1963

‘Bring it Alive’

goldmark

2022

Text: © Andrew Lambirth, 2022
Design: Porter/Goldmark

Art Photographs:
Christian Soro
Sculpture Photographs:
Jay Goldmark

Printed in Wales by Gomer Press

ISBN 978-1-915188-04-5

Andrew Lambirth (born 1959) is a writer, critic and curator. He has written on art for a number of publications including The *Sunday Telegraph*, *The Spectator*, *The Sunday Times*, *Modern Painters* and the *Royal Academy* magazine. Among his many books are monographs on Craigie Aitchison, Roger Hilton, Maggi Hambling, John Hoyland, Margaret Mellis, Allen Jones, LS Lowry, RB Kitaj and Francis Davison. His reviews for *The Spectator* 2002-2014 have been collected in a paperback entitled *A is a Critic*. He has recently completed, in conjunction with Goldmark, a monograph on John Nash.

First published October 2022
Goldmark Gallery, Uppingham
Rutland, LE15 9SQ
01572 821424
goldmarkart.com

inside front cover:
Kneeling Woman with a Bowl, chalk, 1940s, estate stamp, 38 x 28 cm

frontis:
Frank Dobson, late 1920s, courtesy the Dobson Estate

opposite:
Study for Persephone-1, bronze, 1935, estate stamp, 13 x 5 cm
The first casting from the unique terracotta held by the estate

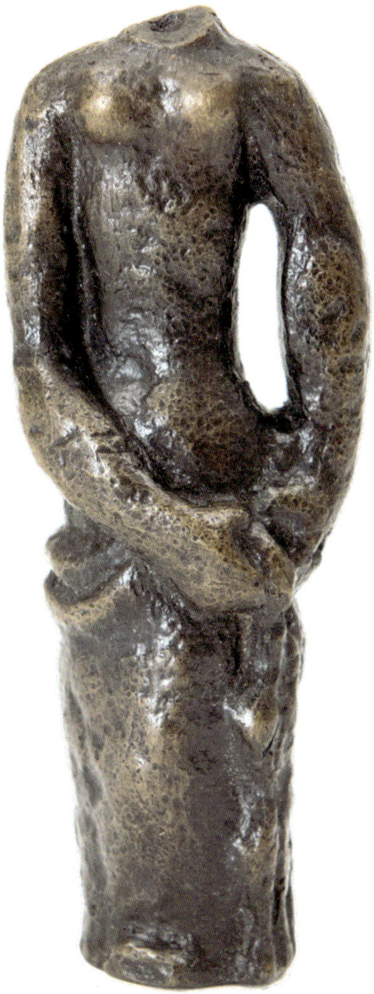

CONTENTS

'make the surface scintillate – bring it alive'.

Frank Dobson to his students at the Royal College of Art

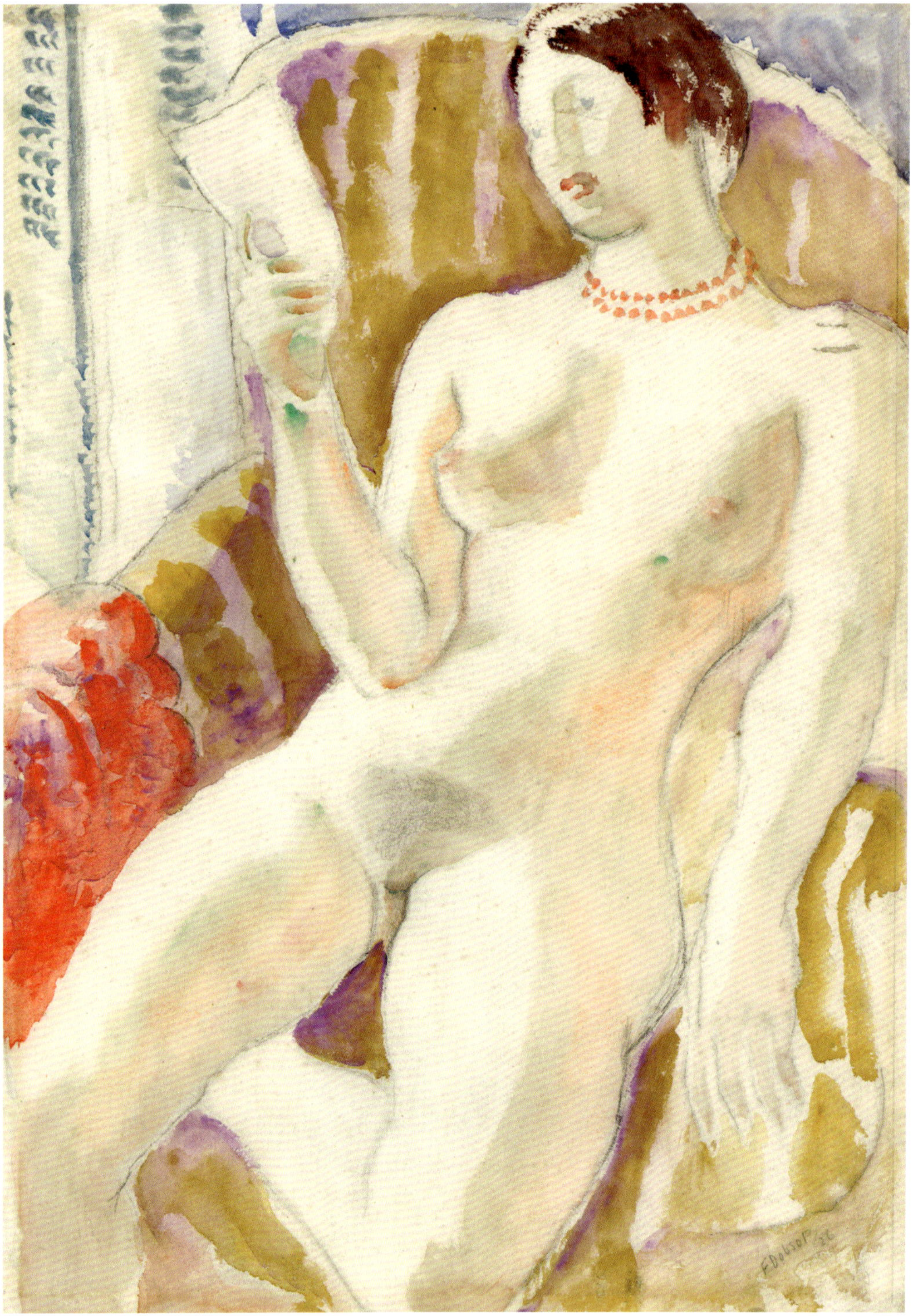

Frank Dobson
Introduction

When Frank Dobson (1886-1963) was growing up, there was very little by way of an indigenous tradition of innovative sculpture in the United Kingdom. There were portrait sculptors and any number of good decorative and applied artists, but Jacob Epstein, Eric Gill and Henri Gaudier-Brzeska appeared like a revelation (and to many a threat) when their work was first seen in this country in the years before WW1. For many, Epstein was too emotionally raw, and too obvious in evoking sexuality. (In France, Rodin was likewise considered too intense.) Gill was equally threatening. So, when Gaudier's career was tragically cut short in the war, Dobson was seen as the acceptable face of modern sculpture. As Roger Fry wrote in October 1925 in *The Burlington Magazine*, Dobson's work was 'true sculpture and pure sculpture', and 'this is almost the first time that such a thing has been even attempted in England.'

Dobson was quickly accepted by many to be Gaudier's natural successor as the leading Modernist sculptor, and thus the champion of the avant-garde. Ezra Pound, for instance, rather embarrassingly introduced him to Hemingway as 'the saviour of sculpture in England'. Did anyone ever ask Dobson if he wanted this poisoned chalice? Of course not. But he was such an easy-going fellow that he accepted what was thrust upon him, enjoyed the adulation when it came in the 1920s and 30s, and didn't seem to mind too much when it receded later on. He was more concerned to make good work and earn a living to support his family.

Yet after his death, Dobson's work went so out of fashion that he was almost forgotten, and the work of rehabilitating his reputation is still going on. The engulfing shadow of Henry Moore (1898-1986) obscured those of his contemporaries less successful at self-promotion, and Moore himself was not especially generous about the achievements of others. (One critic was surprised to hear him denigrate Barbara Hepworth on the day her death was announced.) Instead of due

The Reader, watercolour, 1926, signed, 49 x 34 cm

attention being given to the debt that later artists like Moore and Hepworth owed to Dobson, his work has been passed over. Dismissed as a 'vernacular modernist', he has too often been pigeonholed as a follower of the French classicist Aristide Maillol (1861-1944).

That's a lazy characterisation based on an apparent similarity of look. Dobson liked Maillol's work and admired the artist, but he did not emulate him. A bigger influence on Dobson was the primitivism of Gauguin. Maillol's work can be traced back to the Greeks and Romans in a conscious connection with the traditions of Antiquity. Rodin admired the uncomplicated appeal of some of his sculptures, which, he said, made no attempt to arouse curiosity, being so clearly about beauty and purity. Revealingly, Maillol was overshadowed by Rodin, much as Dobson was overshadowed by Moore. Brancusi referred to Rodin's influence as 'like the shadow of a great tree'.

Leaving aside for one moment those overpowering talents and great swollen egos, Rodin and Moore, it is often possible to learn more about the temper and beliefs of an age by examining those artists whose reputations have risen and fallen with changes in taste and fashion. Frank Dobson is one such, whose career can teach us a great deal about the 1920s and 1930s in particular. He was an important transitional figure in the history of British sculpture, and, in the museum curator Robert Hopper's words, 'one of the most interesting to be found in British art of the period 1915 to 1945.'

Dobson was six years younger than Epstein and 12 years older than Moore, and, as such, occupied a key historical position. However, it was his grave misfortune that his early career was to be utterly disrupted by WW1. He had his first solo exhibition (of paintings and drawings) in 1914, but, discovering his true metier as a sculptor, had already started to carve in wood. By 1915 he was poised to launch his career as a sculptor, and wanted desperately to do so. Yet he found himself volunteering to fight in the army, and by the time he was invalided out in 1918, the world had changed and so had he. The war had exacted a heavy toll, and Dobson was never really to regain his health.

Both Moore and Hepworth owe a debt to Dobson in their early work, though it is rarely acknowledged. For instance, Dobson was drawing on pre-Columbian carving in 1915, over a decade before Moore decided this was his territory and his alone. And Dobson's seated and reclining figures of the 1920s do seem to pave

Morning, bronze, 2021, ed 12, estate stamp, h 23 cm
Cast from the 1925 bronze

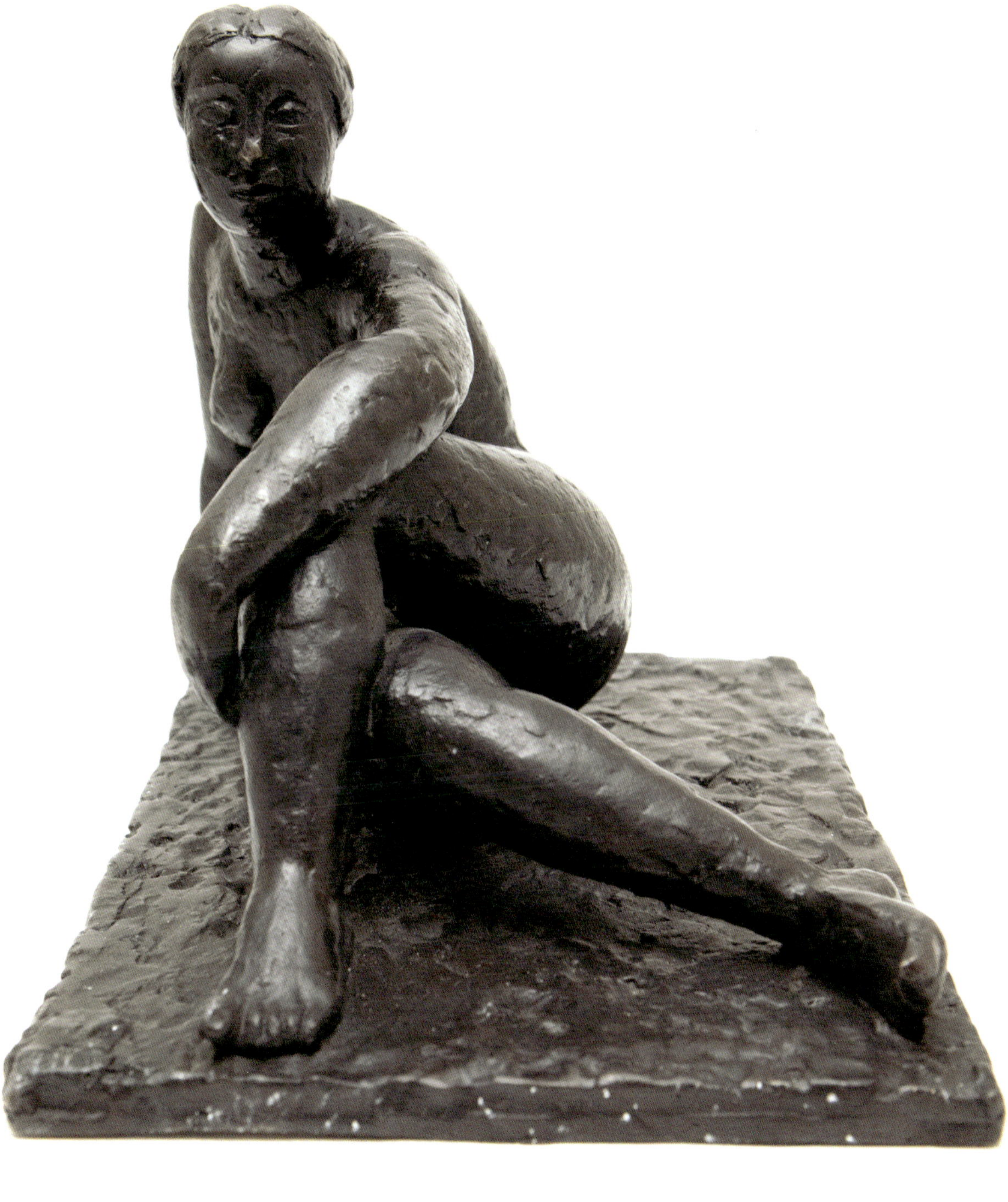

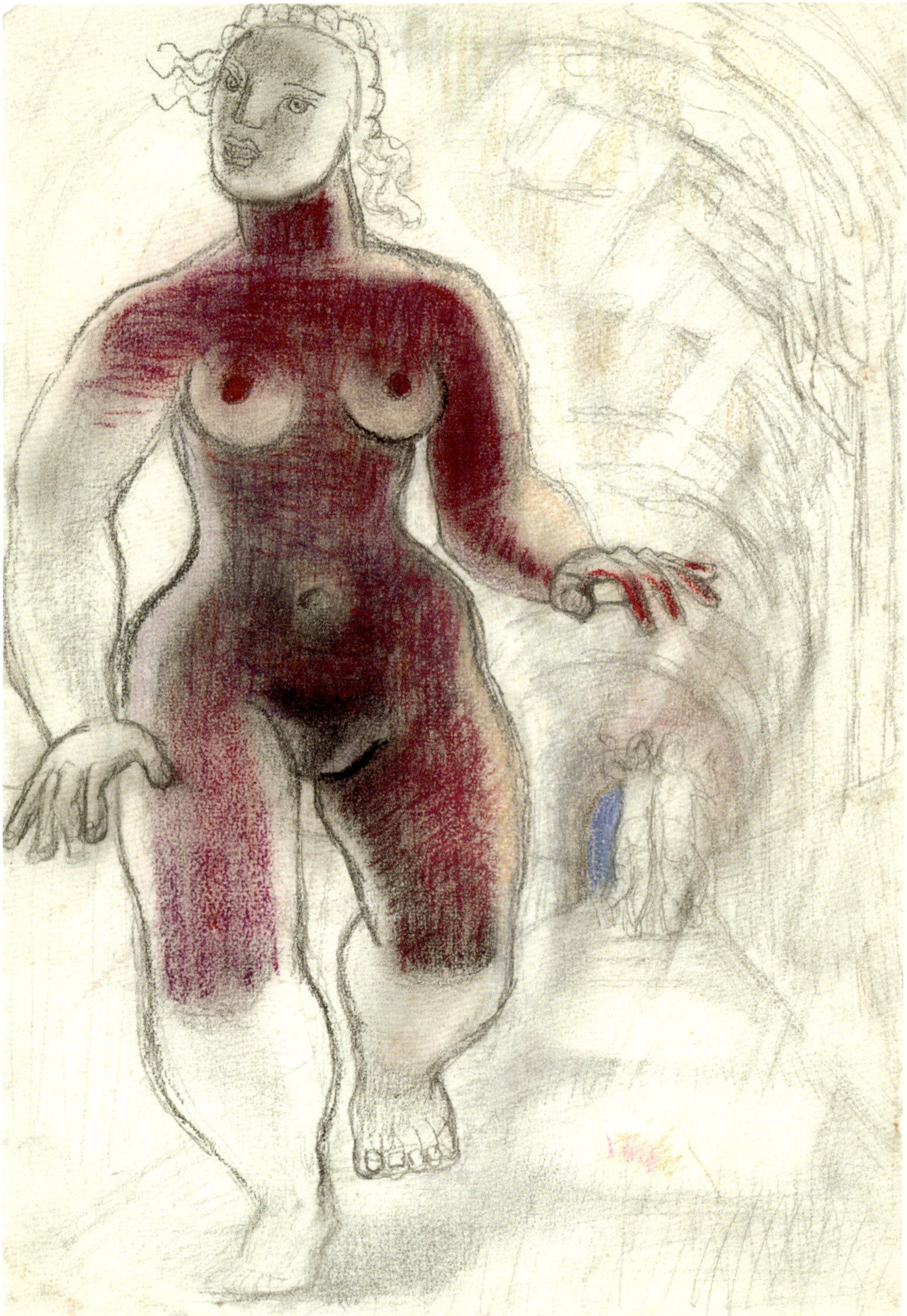

the way for Moore's own development — not that the latter would ever admit it. One of the problems was that Dobson's work was never as spectacular as Moore's or Hepworth's, despite its contained rhythmic power.

Dobson believed the sculptor should be versatile, able to turn his hand equally to carving or modelling. This accords with his firm belief in craftsmanship, learned as a trainee apprentice in the studio of Sir William Reynolds-Stephens. Dobson was convinced that there was no difference between carving and modelling, both were techniques or skills available to the trained sculptor. Likewise he didn't make much distinction between drawing an apple and drawing a person. 'It's all drawing', he said, 'and, to me, mainly the study of form.'

His beliefs cut right across the impassioned debate which raged in the 1920s and 30s between direct carving on one side and modelling on the other. Dobson maintained that there was no fundamental difference between them, that it was all working in three dimensions. He stated categorically: 'I hate all this pedantry that makes a clear-cut distinction between carving stone and modelling clay. There isn't one for the sculptor.'

He was more interested in a search for

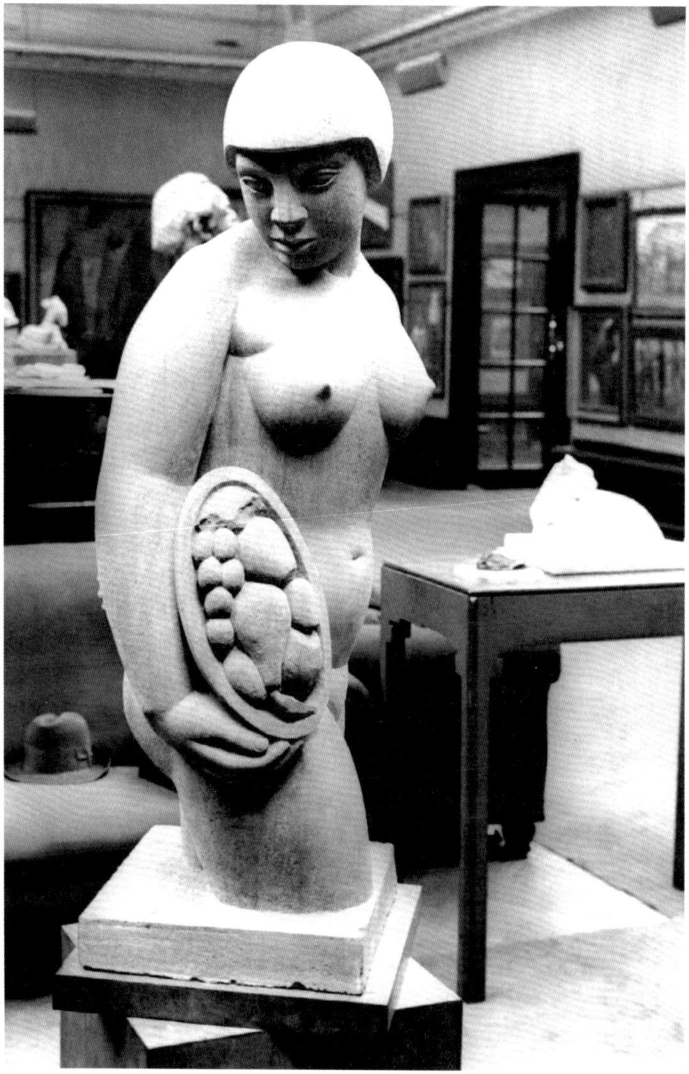

Walking Nude, chalk & pencil, estate stamp verso, 35.5 x 25.5 cm
Cornucopia, stone, 1925-7, University of Hull

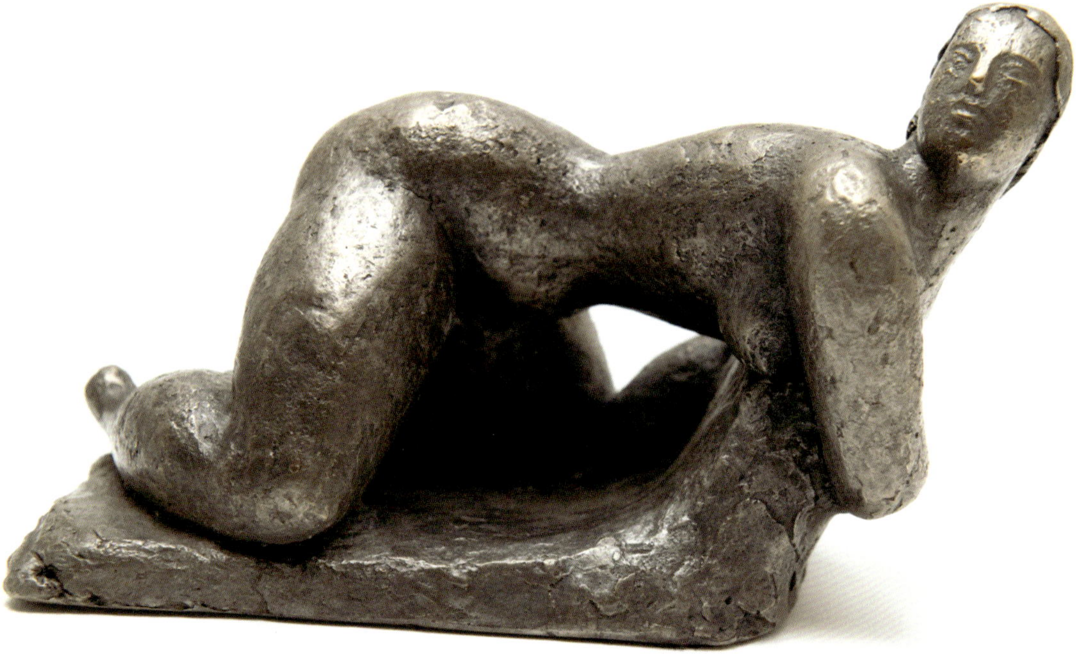

harmony, and with conveying to his viewers the spiritual and aesthetic pleasure of his work. His sculptures are vivid with life, but also sought stability and formal completeness. His work engaged with emotion, but was not tortured in any way, moving more towards serenity than anguish. Art was a sanctuary from the chaos of life, and he loved swelling and ebbing forms, oceanic in their grandeur. Dobson had an eye for a full set of curves, and depicted his women accordingly. The Dobson Girl is the archetypal female: mother, daughter, sister, lover, wife. Dobson's embodiments of the archetype are depicted with empathy, affection and generosity.

Dobson's women tend to be of the earth, rooted as hills or mountains. Ironically, limbs like tree trunks and knees like boulders have never seemed to count against Henry Moore, though when Dobson employed a similar weightiness of physique it was held against him by some

Crawling Woman, bronze, 2021, ed 12, estate stamp, h 15 cm
Cast from the 1944 terracotta
Persephone, watercolour & gouache, 1930s, signed, 62.4 x 47.5 cm

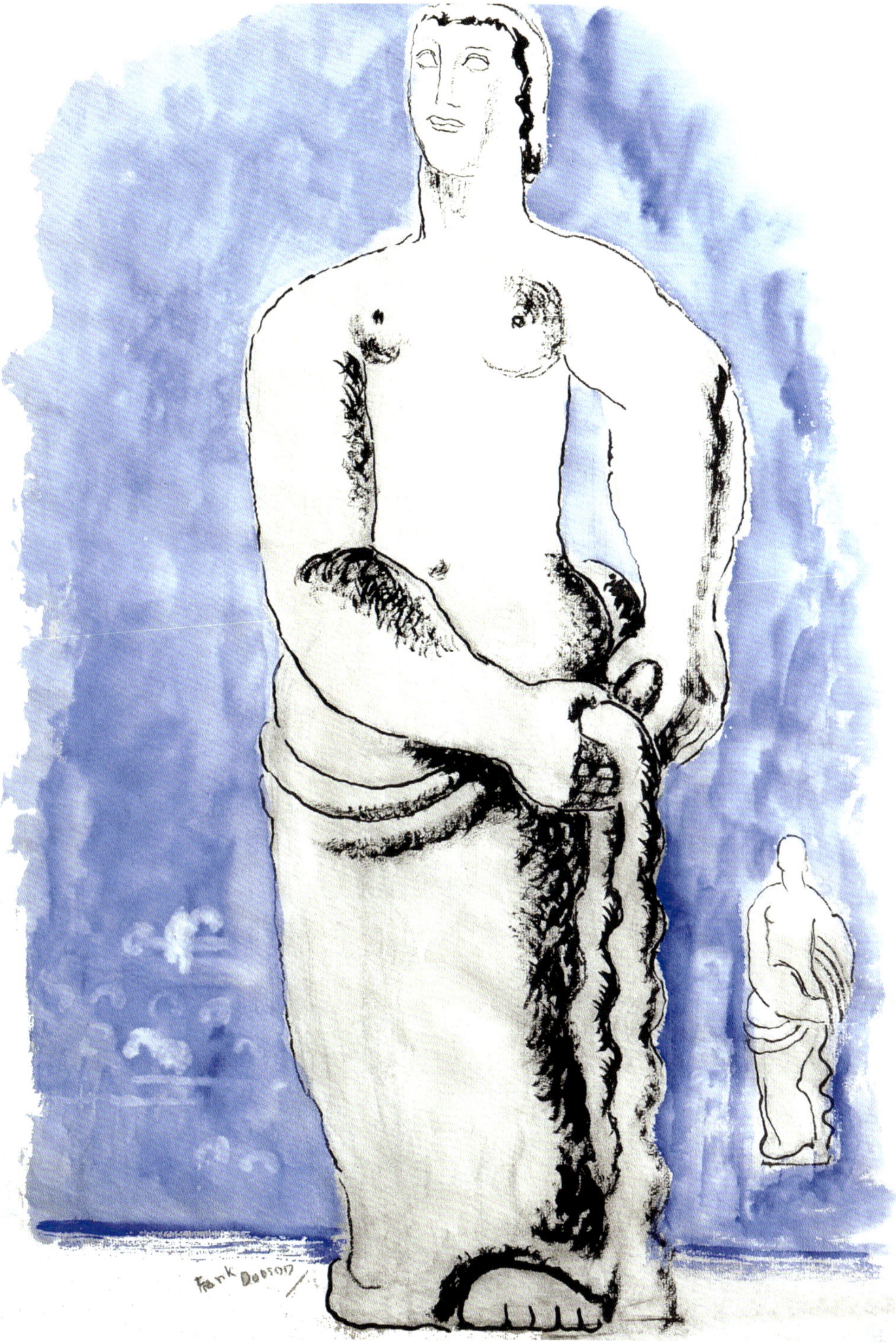
Frank Dobson

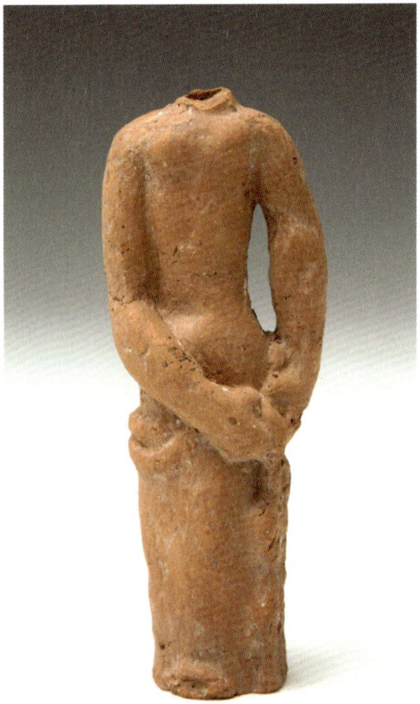

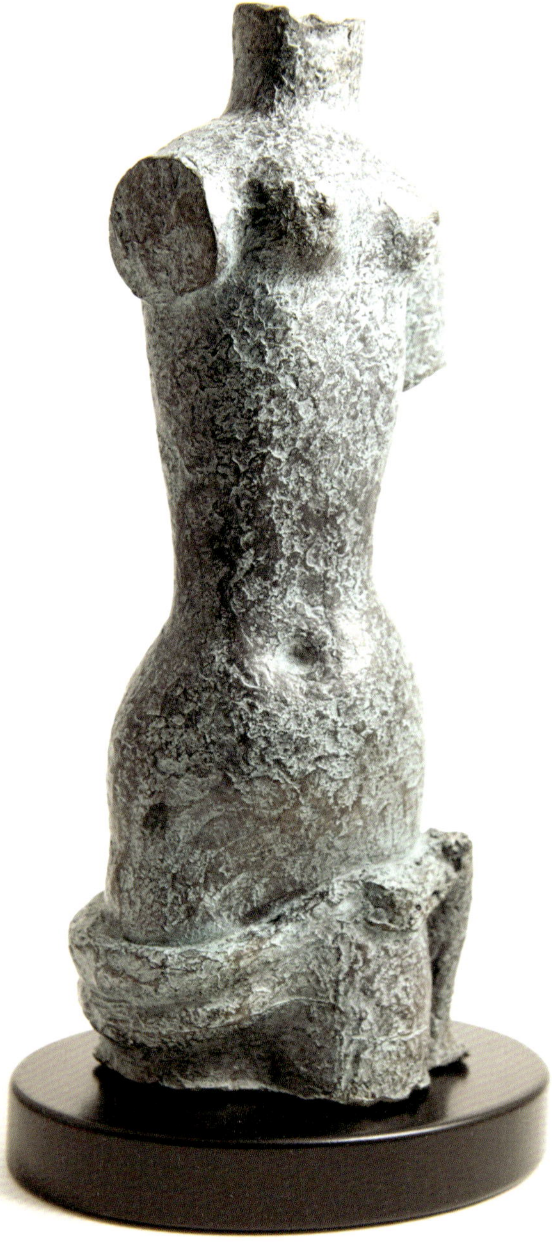

commentators. Is it because Dobson's work is more involved with sexuality, however demure in the exhibited work? Moore's figures are rarely considered for their sex appeal; Dobson's are.

Dobson didn't want to dismember or distort the body as so many sculptors and painters did. His forms are sometimes accentuated rather than strictly naturalistic, but always in the search for truth as he saw it. He was inventing all the time, making shapes that worked three-dimensionally as primal sculptural forms. Neither academic nor conventional, he was a man of good sense, not assertive or self-publicising, a painter turned sculptor, which was an acceptable career trajectory, shared with Degas, Gauguin, Picasso and Matisse. There is a fundamental and unquenchable optimism to his work, which is primarily about pleasure and contentment and beauty.

He described his procedure in a 1933 interview. His practice was first to make a maquette in clay or wax, even when carving in stone. This would represent several months of thinking about a sculpture. 'Having found the form, I then have to decide on the scale on which it is to be made.' Only at that point would he draw from a life model, researching every aspect of the pose, making anything from a dozen studies to as many as a hundred. This isn't unusual for a sculptor: Picasso, for instance, made around a hundred drawings to establish the pose of his 1943 sculpture *Man with a Lamb*. They say that genius is an infinite capacity for taking pains.

It was Dobson's belief that: 'The primary appeal of sculpture is to the emotion which results from contemplating the peculiar and apparently static evolutions which take place when a number of forms are superbly assembled.' Dobson was just such a superb assembler of forms, who aimed at stillness. But there is always movement of forms within the whole, which constitutes rhythm. (His rhythmic treatment of mass owed something to his study of African sculpture.) This is the balancing of parts so essential to the creation of a satisfying unity.

An anecdote told by a sculptor of a later generation is revealing. Anthony Caro recalled a visit to his London studio during the 1960s from the influential American critic Clement Greenberg, and the two of them spending the day together looking at art and art books. At one point Greenberg came across a book illustrating a Henry Moore on one page and a Dobson opposite. Caro remembered Greenberg pointing to the Dobson and saying: 'That is the better sculpture.'

Study for Persephone 1, terracotta, 1935, h 13 cm
Standing Torso (Study for Persephone 3), bronze, 2021, ed 12, estate stamp, h 36 cm
First casting from the 1935 unique terracotta

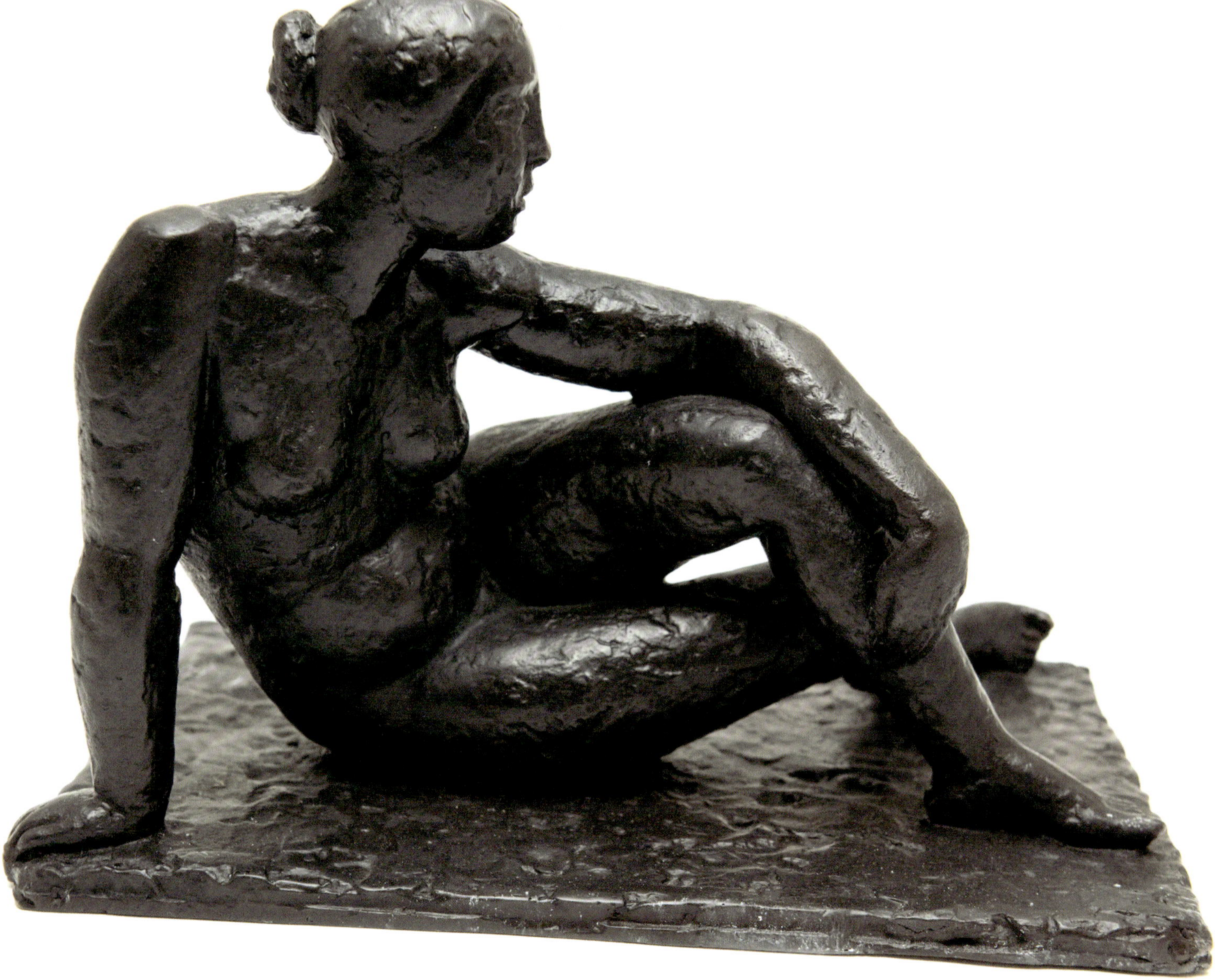

2

The Making of a Sculptor and the First World War (1886-1919)

Morning, bronze, 2021, ed 12, estate stamp, h 23 cm
Cast from the 1925 bronze

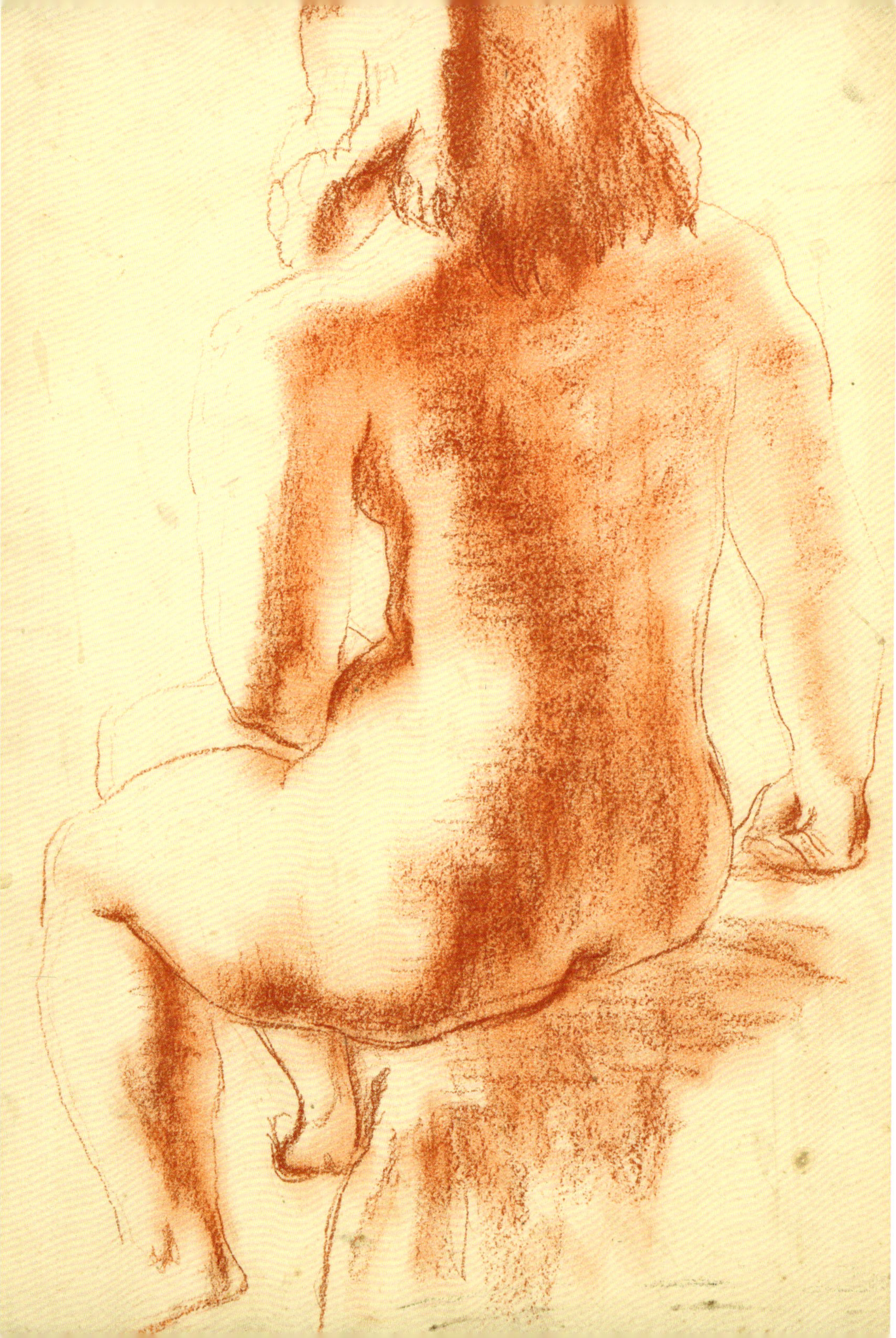

'I think I can say quite fairly that ever since I can remember, I have known about art.'

Frank Dobson

Frank Dobson was born on 18th November 1886 at Queen Charlotte's Maternity Hospital in London, at that time situated in the Marylebone Road. The family lived in Acton Street, King's Cross, and art surrounded the young boy from his earliest years. Frank's father, Frank Dobson senior, was an artist, though on his 1878 marriage certificate to Eliza Brooks, he is described as an artist's colourman. A colourman makes and mixes colours and sells them, which would suggest that he was in the paint supply business before becoming an artist himself. For Frank senior was a journeyman artist specialising in painting flowers and birds, mainly for the Christmas card market. Young Frank duly went on sketching expeditions with his father and was first taken to the British Museum and National Gallery by him, aged five or six.

By the age of eight Frank was grinding his father's colours for his paintings, and clearly had an early understanding of an artist's materials. One piece of wisdom Frank senior passed on to his son was his notion of the hierarchy of art. He said that what he did was Art, what the Academicians at the Royal Academy did was High Art, and what was in the National Gallery was Great Art. In his pursuit of great art, aged 11 Frank junior won a scholarship to Leyton School of Art, then known as Leyton Technical School, which he attended while still a schoolboy for two mornings and five evenings a week.

Then, when he was 14, tragedy struck and his father died. Young Frank ran away from home, sleeping in doorways and railway arches until taken in by an aunt in Hastings. There was clearly no love lost between Frank and his mother and all connection was severed. He studied briefly at Hastings School of Art but, realising he had to take a job to support himself, applied for the post of apprentice studio boy to the fashionable sculptor Sir William Reynolds-Stephens (1862-1943). Reynolds-Stephens was one of the more original artists of the New Sculpture in the late 19th century, which mixed enhanced naturalism

Back of Seated Nude, red chalk, estate stamp verso, 45.5 x 30.5 cm

with surface decoration. (Alfred Gilbert was another.)

Dobson spent a year and a half with Reynolds-Stephens, who was essentially a decorative sculptor, taking his subjects mainly from the poems of Tennyson. Dobson received a training in Art Nouveau applied art and design, which did little to satisfy his artistic needs and instincts but gave him a lifelong appreciation of proper craftsmanship. He could see no future for himself in such a milieu, so decided to leave the security of Reynolds-Stephens' studio and went down to Devon to paint watercolours of the landscape to earn his keep.

He did not remain long in Devon, moving on to Newquay in Cornwall where he spent a couple of years (1904-6), again painting for a living, producing work that would sell instantly, rather than possess any intrinsic artistic merit. These potboilers were painted under two assumed names, Tom Newbold and Evelyn Bishop, and Dobson clearly drew on the experience of watching his father, and set up a production line. He painted in watercolour exclusively, mostly landscapes of the seashore or Highland cattle on the moors, anything that would be saleable. He did a brisk trade to furniture shops for £1 a picture.

At this time, an amateur artist befriended him and told him of scholarships available to study at another art school, Hospitalfield in Arbroath, on the east coast of Scotland. Dobson sent up examples of his work and duly won a scholarship. So began what he later acknowledged to be the most formative period of his life. The core of the teaching was life drawing, and if the drawing method was old fashioned (stump drawing with a paper cylinder to blend charcoal marks to achieve the tonal values of the figure), he was nevertheless to benefit from it considerably. To begin with, he learnt about *form* by doing so much life drawing, and this was essential to his later development as a sculptor. And even some of his mature drawings reveal in their evocative smudging this early training.

At Hospitalfield he also spent a lot of his spare time drawing from reproductions of Old Masters, almost in secret, for this was not encouraged. But Dobson was eager to learn by example, and copied Rembrandt, Michelangelo, Holbein and the red chalk drawings of Alfred Stevens (1817-75), the British sculptor. Dobson later described him as 'the only recent sculptor whose drawings showed something of the quality of which I was in search'. The other revelation was painting in oils for the first time. Although he was supposed

Woman Peeling an Apple (The Bastard), oil on canvas, 1913, 65 x 56 cm

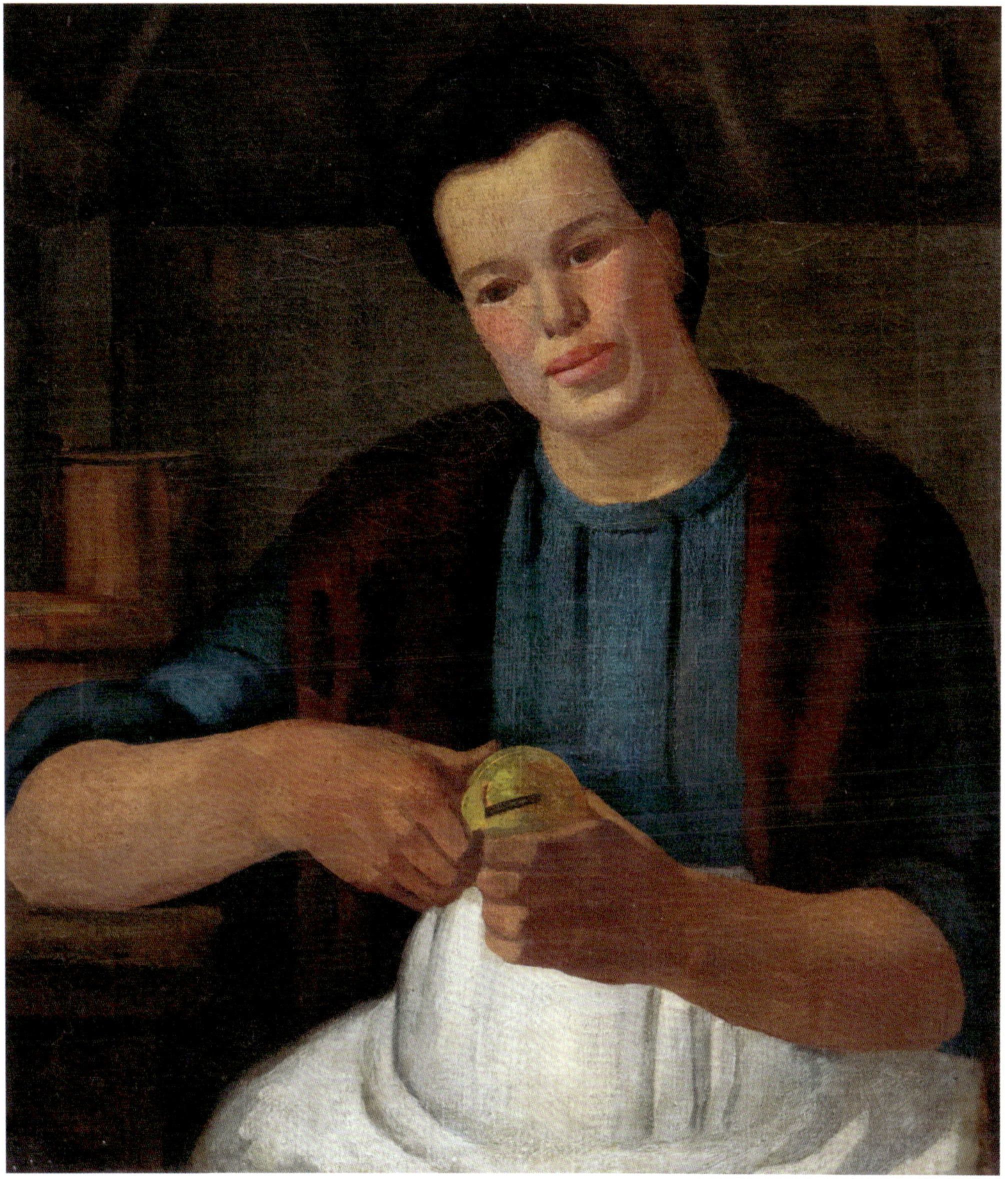

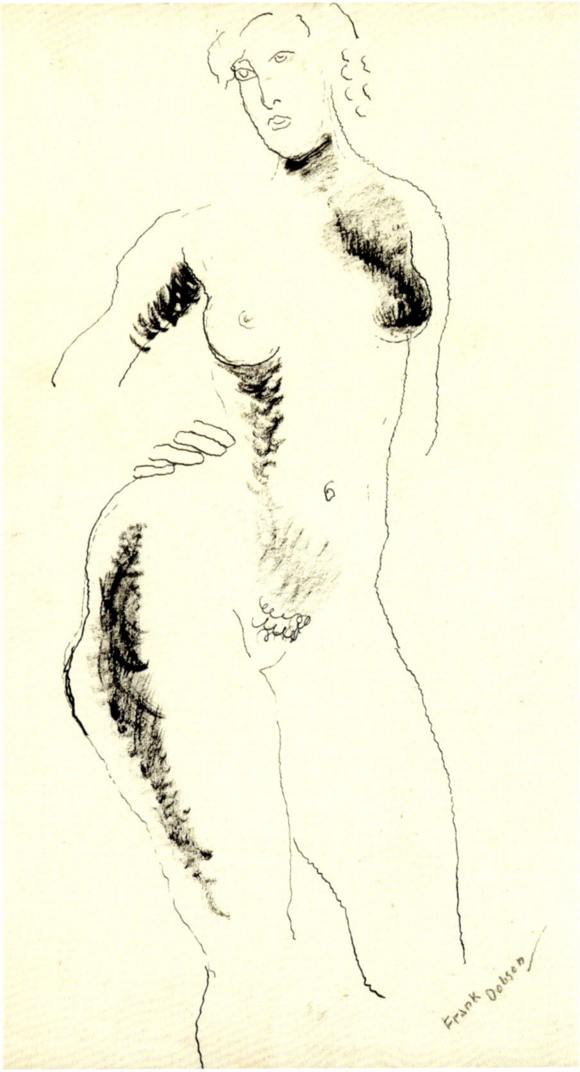

to paint figures, it took him a long time to master the new medium (all his previous skill had been focused on watercolour), and to do so he concentrated on painting landscape, particularly trees. He also saw more modern art, being introduced to the Impressionists for the first time at The Royal Institute for the Fine Arts in Glasgow; he was especially impressed by Monet and Pissarro.

In 1910 he completed his four year course, and after graduating from Hospitalfield he relocated to London, painting by day and continuing to attend art school in the evenings and on Saturdays. This was the City & Guilds, then known as the South London School of Technical Art. The 1910s were a period of artistic ferment, largely occasioned by Roger Fry's two Post-Impressionist exhibitions, in 1910 and 1912. These were immensely important to Dobson, who wrote of their eye-opening effect. 'Anything was possible. Here was something more than just emotion. Here was work for the intelligence.' Afterwards he said he chiefly remembered two artists: Cézanne and Gauguin, to whom he was drawn by their depiction of essential form and volume. (Although Brancusi and Maillol were also represented, revealingly they left little trace on him.)

Hand on Hip, pen & ink, signed, 51 x 23 cm

If looking at the Impressionists had liberated Dobson's sense of colour, the Post-Impressionists spoke to him of form, though Gauguin's exotic palette was also to leave its mark on Dobson. Remembering back, Dobson said that Gauguin's work sent him off to the British Museum to look again at 'Negro' sculpture, Peruvian, Egyptian and Assyrian art. Later, when recuperating in hospital from injuries and illness sustained in WW1, Dobson asked his friend Eddie Marsh to lend him some reproductions of Gauguin's work.

As a painter, Dobson particularly admired among English artists the work of Augustus John and Mark Gertler. Inevitably, his own efforts reflected their influence, so it is no surprise that when John saw the young Dobson's paintings he encouraged him to exhibit and opened the way for his first solo show at the Chenil Galleries in Chelsea. This was to take place in 1914. Just before that, Dobson was in Cornwall again (1913-14), where he shared a studio in Newlyn with Cedric Morris, painting mostly portraits. *Portrait of a Young Girl* in the Atkinson Art Gallery, Southport, tentatively dated to 1917 but more likely 1914, or even 1911, is a good example from this period.

Meanwhile, in 1915 he made his first wood carving. In retrospect, he identified the impulses

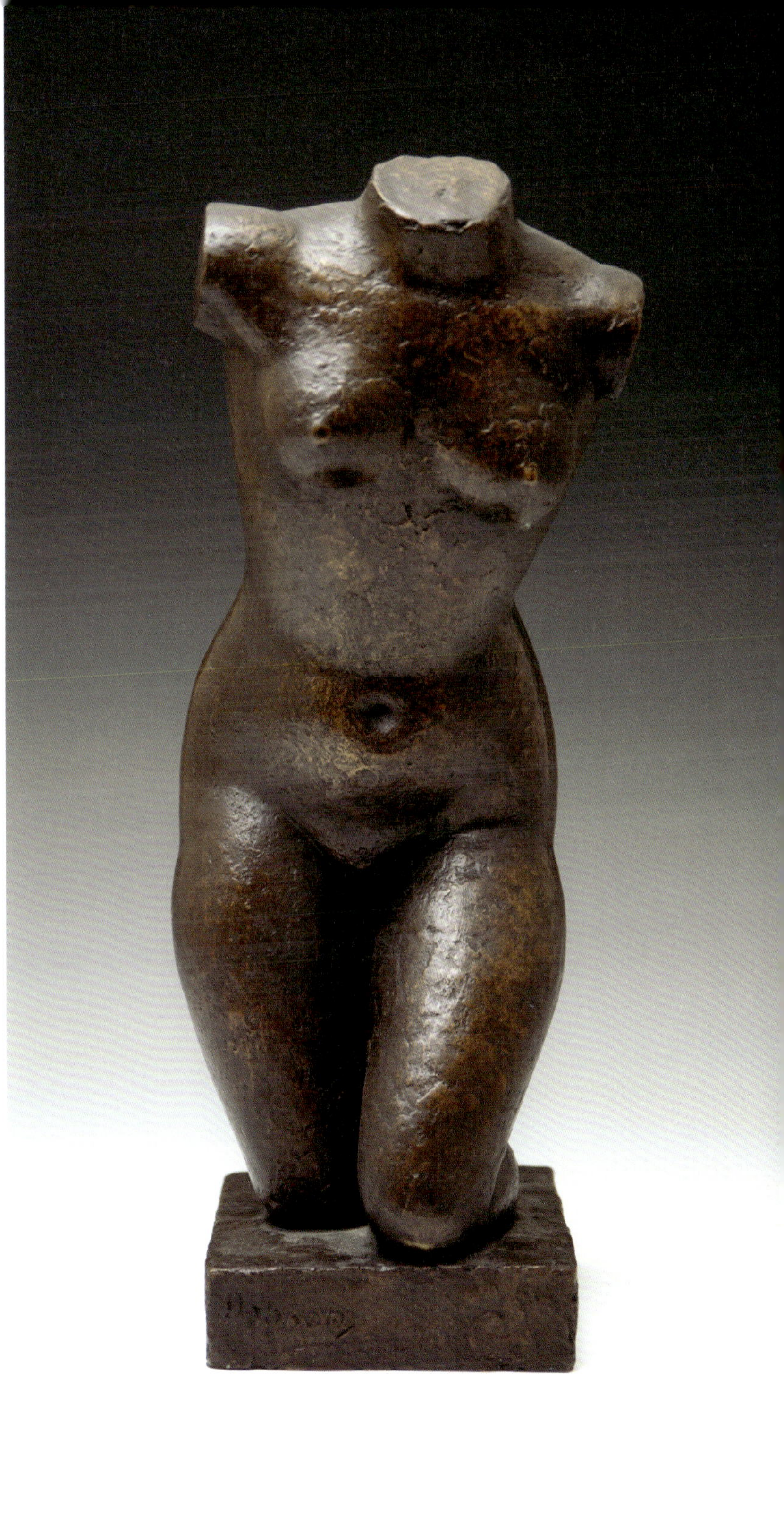

Kneeling Torso, bronze, 2021, ed 12, signed, h 46 cm
Cast from the 1928 bronze

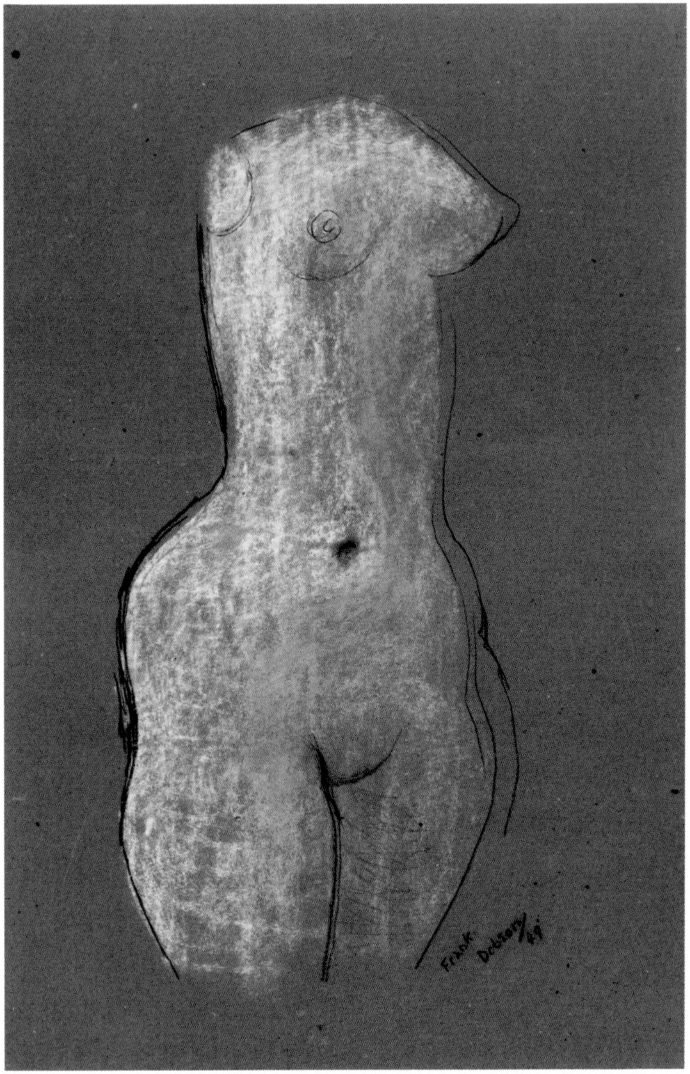

that drove him in the direction of sculpture: 'I found that in painting, the results were achieved too soon.' He realised he wanted 'to go further and do more.' Drawing clearly played a key role in this move. Dobson commented: 'It was while looking at one of my figure drawings that I decided to do my first piece of sculpture.' He took up a piece of oak and carved *Seated Female Nude*, somewhat indebted stylistically to Gauguin, and soon followed it by his first stone carving, *Kneeling Female Figure*, in sandstone.

Although he was now making sculpture, his 1914 Chenil Galleries exhibition had consisted entirely of drawings and paintings. He would need to spend more time working in three dimensions before he felt sufficiently confident of his new work to show it publicly, but he was making such good progress that this could well have been in a matter of months, rather than years. Dobson sold well at the Chenil exhibition, and met one of the most ubiquitous patrons and collectors of the time, Edward (Eddie) Marsh. The introduction was made by the artist John Currie, who generously wrote to Marsh in support of Dobson's work. Marsh was to remain a firm friend and supporter.

In 1915 Dobson volunteered to serve in the army, and saw active service with the Artists'

Nude Torso, chalk, 1949, signed, 56.5 x 38 cm
Elsie Queen Myers (Head), painted plaster, 1921, h 23 cm

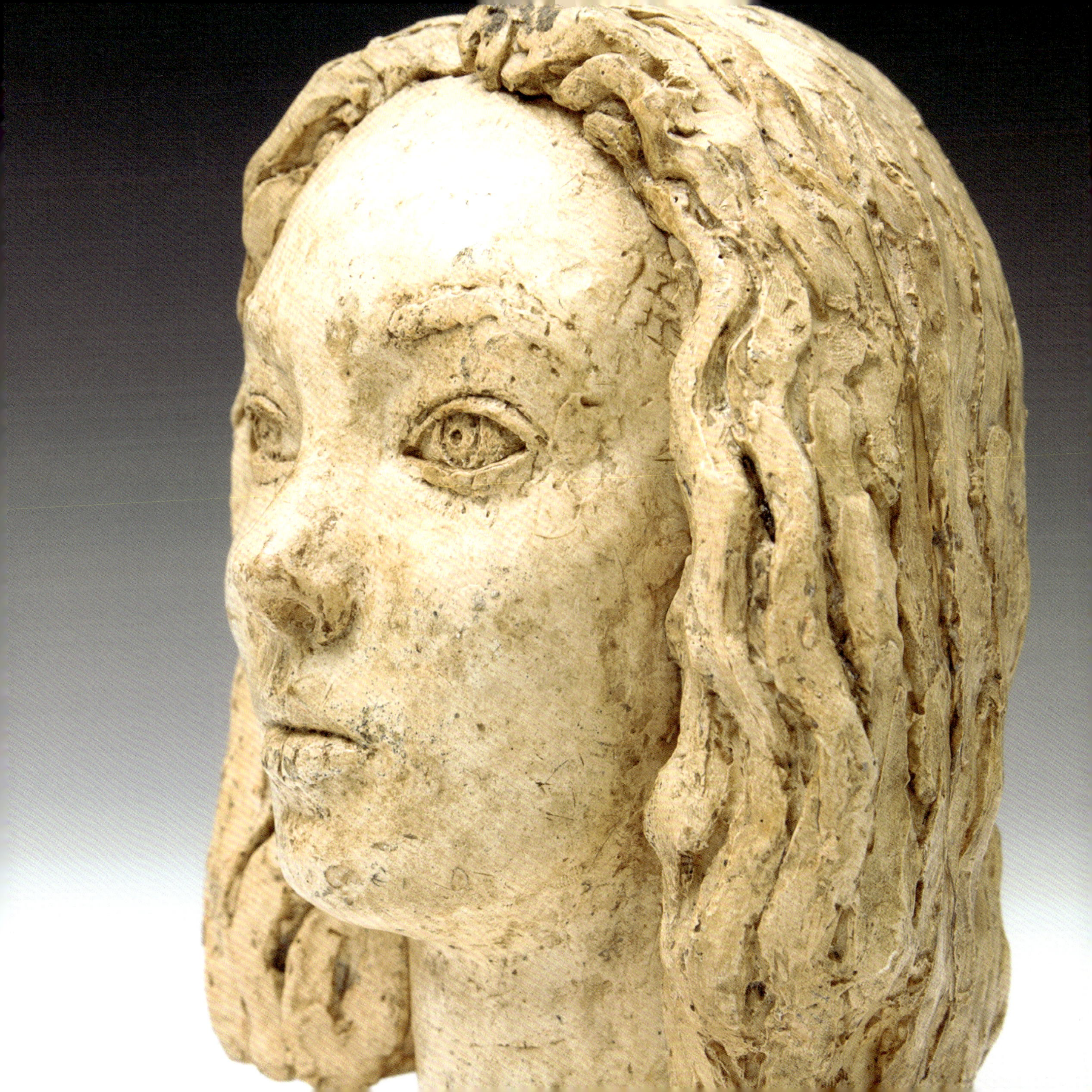

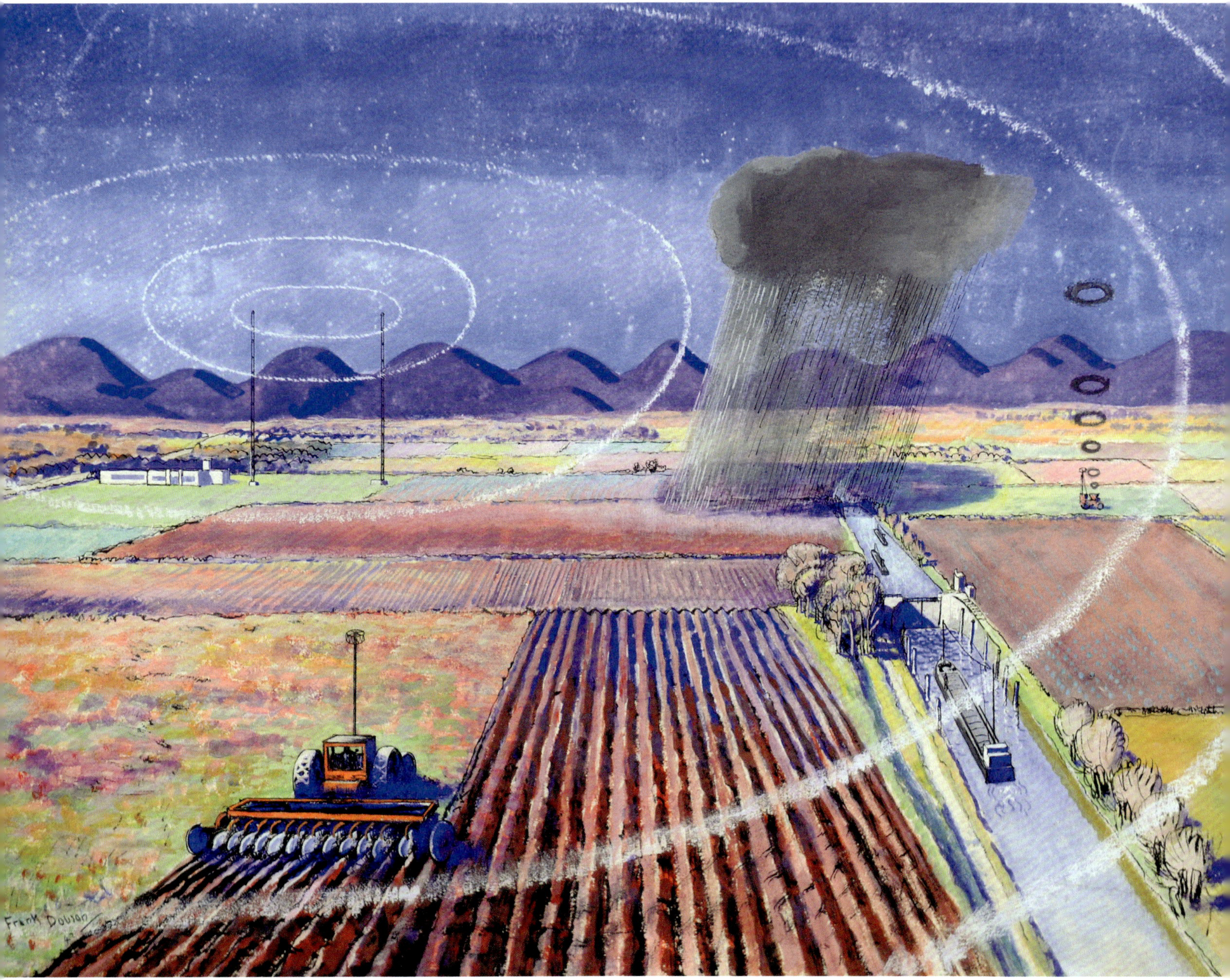

Rifles in France. Although it was a duodenal ulcer that was responsible for him being invalided out in November 1918, he also suffered in the front line. He was blown up and sent back to England suffering from shell shock, and one account held that he was buried twice in one day by shelling. His friend Wyndham Lewis wrote in his war memoir, *Blasting and Bombardiering*: 'There was Frank Dobson, the sculptor, who had been blown up by a mine in France, and looked as if he had, what's more...'

In the army Dobson had had little chance to practise his art, but when he came out he at once sought commissions. *The Balloon Apron* (1918, Imperial War Museum) is his finest exercise in war art, a rare oil on canvas and a powerful image, mostly of sky and the smoke from factory chimneys soaring into the evening blue, with an apron screen of barrage balloons featuring almost incidentally. Apron screens consisted of three balloons 500 yards apart, joined by a heavy steel cable, with an almost invisible net hanging between them, intended to deter enemy aircraft.

Here the big dramatic sky is the key factor, rather as it is in John Nash's *Oppy Wood* of the same year, also in the Imperial War Museum. The farmland below the sky is flat: reclaimed Essex marshes, with plump-headed trees, a strong composition painted in potent colour. But Dobson's style perturbed the officials — art would keep breaking in — and he received a letter of complaint. 'The smoke and sky seemed to worry the Committee and if these effects could be subdued they would be glad.' How much of Dobson's original vision has survived it is now difficult to tell; let us hope he ignored the philistines and stuck to his convictions.

In 1919, Dobson joined X Group at Lewis' instigation, and became the only sculptor in this association of painters which was trying to recapture the radical stance of pre-war Vorticism. Conceived as an alternative exhibiting body to the London Group, X Group included William Roberts, Edward Wadsworth and McKnight Kauffer, the celebrated poster designer, among its members. X Group (as Lewis himself called it, though it is more usually known at Group X) held only one exhibition, in 1920 at Heal's, and quite failed to re-establish the militant avant-garde mentality that Lewis had hoped for. After that brief cooperative involvement, Dobson was allowed to make his way on his own.

Farm with Rain Cloud and Radiowave, gouache, ink & chalk, 1942, signed, 49.5 x 64.7 cm

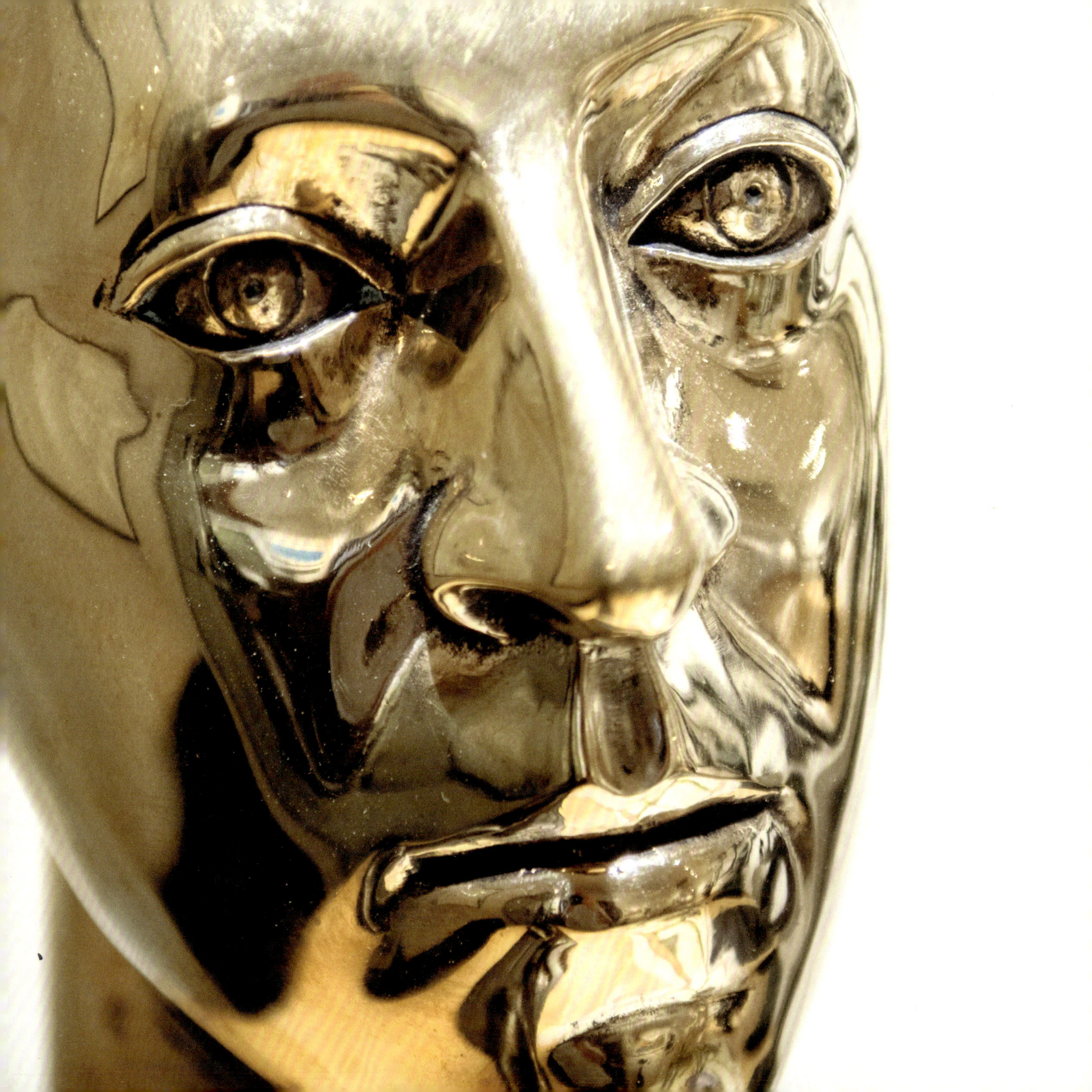

3

Peace & Fame (1920-30)

Sir Osbert Sitwell (detail), polished bronze, 2022, ed 3, estate stamp, h 32 cm
Cast from the 1922 plaster

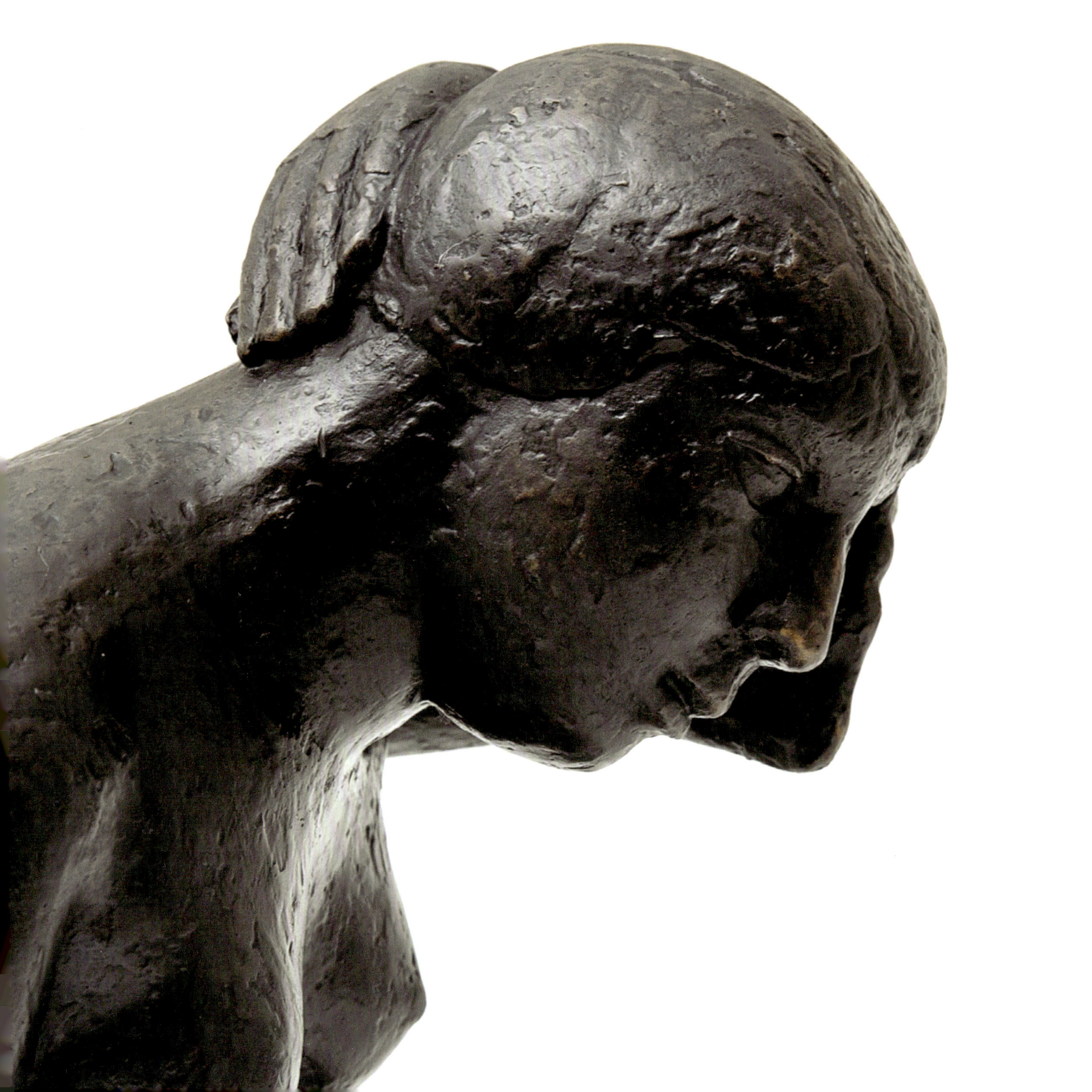

'One must interpret.'

Frank Dobson

Ben Nicholson was one of the first friends Dobson made after the war. They met in 1919, and visited Newlyn together that summer when Dobson made a plaster portrait bust of Nicholson (present whereabouts unknown), which was shown at the Leicester Galleries in November 1925. There is also a conté and gouache drawing of Nicholson from the same year. This was an important friendship for Nicholson, who changed his own style almost overnight, ditching the elegant versions of his father's still-life paintings he had been doing for something altogether more radical. In fact, Nicholson attributed great significance to Dobson's example, listing him with such greats as Blake, Memling and Matisse as crucial influences on him. In a letter of March 1923 Nicholson wrote: 'I think that Bomberg and Dobson remain the only 2 people in England that are convincing in their efforts to get at a big & universal outlook...'

Clearly Dobson was a catalyst for Nicholson, enabling him to make a break from his father's dominance. There was also a personal aspect to this influence and rivalry, in that William Nicholson stole his son's girlfriend, Edith Stuart-Wortley, and married her in 1919. Nicholson needed friends to help him come to terms with this family drama, and both Dobson and his first wife Cordelia were sympathetic. Nicholson's studio at Cheyne Walk was close to the Dobsons at Trafalgar Studios in Manresa Road, and they were happy to be friendly and hospitable. Later, when Dobson's marriage to Cordelia collapsed and he took a new wife in 1926, loyalties were tested, and the friendship between the artists faded out. But for a while, Dobson was close to Ben, though ironically he seems to have got on equally well with his father, William.

Meanwhile Dobson was concerned mostly with developing his sculpture and in 1921 held his first solo exhibition at the Leicester Galleries — the first of eight according to Oliver Brown, the gallery's chronicler. (Dobson had already exhibited there in a mixed show with the Artists'

Woman Seated (detail), bronze, 2019, ed 10, signed, h 38 cm
Cast from the 1926 bronze

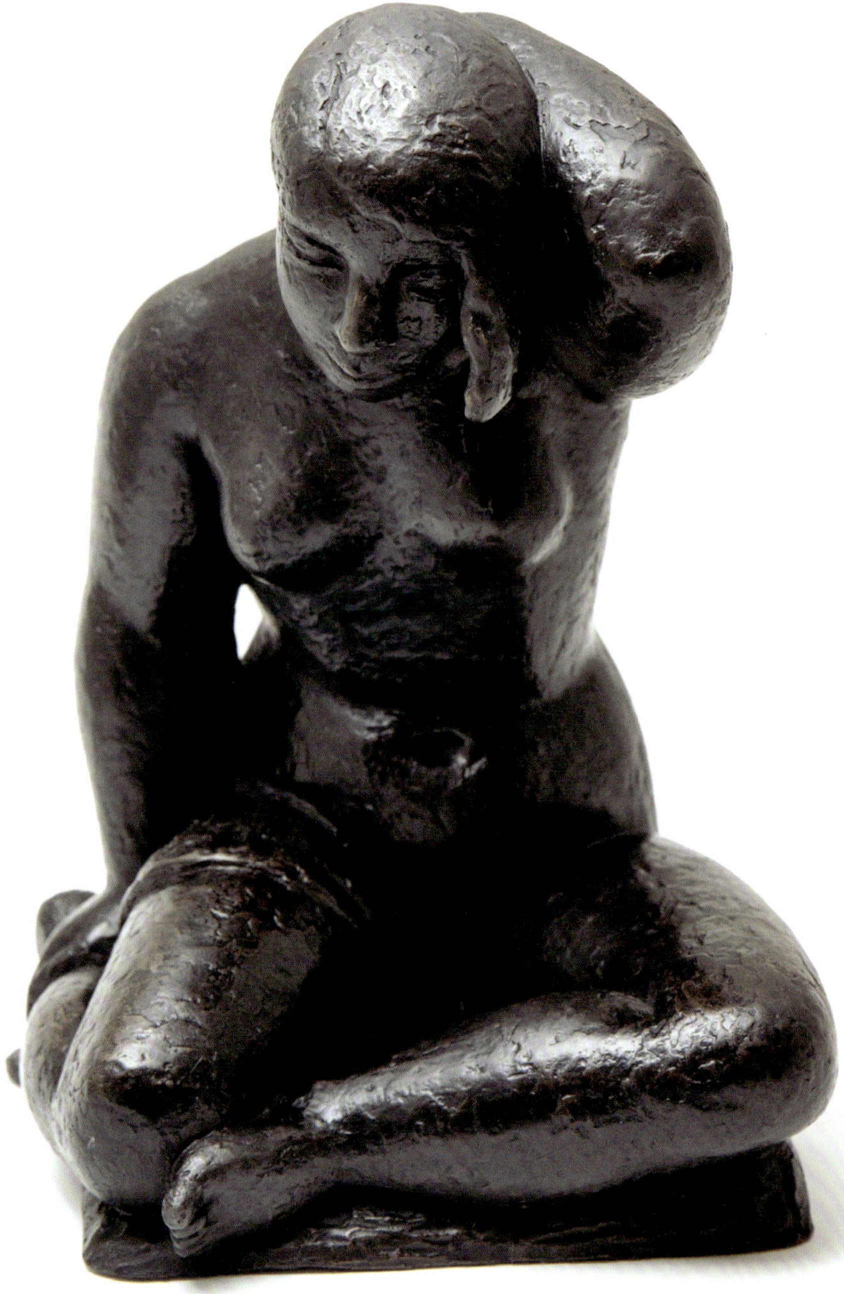

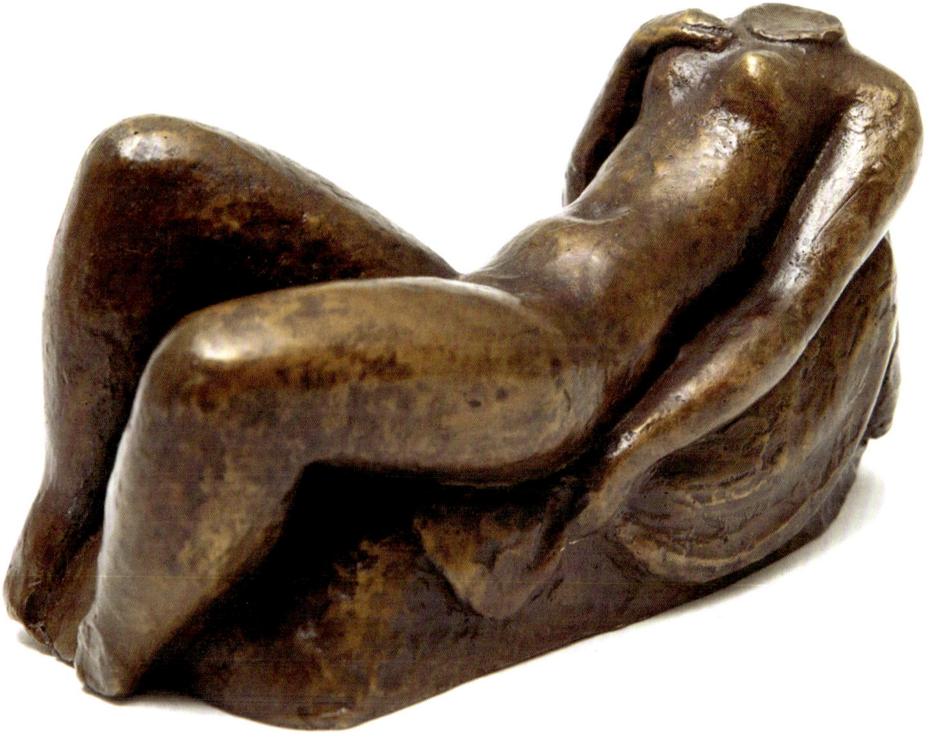

Rifles in 1916, but this was his first solo show as a sculptor.) It was this exhibition which effectively began the process of registering him in the art public's consciousness as a sculptor, even while his understanding of his materials and what he could do with them continued to develop. Dobson remained open to other influences and inspirations, and his first trip to Paris in 1922 was particularly eventful in this respect.

The trip was undertaken with Stephen Tomlin, Dobson's Bloomsbury friend and private sculpture pupil, at which time he saw much that was to have resonance with him: a display of African sculpture and important collections of Oriental porcelain; also an exhibition of bathers by Picasso at Paul Rosenberg's gallery. The influence of these figures on Dobson was in one respect an affirmation of his own direction,

Woman Seated (detail), bronze, 2019, ed 10, signed, h 38 cm
Cast from the 1926 bronze
Recumbent Nude, bronze, 2018, ed 10, stamped signature, 8 x 16 cm
The first cast from the 1925 plaster

though the approach of each artist was so different. Picasso's neo-classical women of 1920 and 1921 are solid through and through, monumental, with no waists to speak of. Dobson gave his girls very defined waists to emphasise and enhance their ultra-feminine attributes and charms. It was at this time that Dobson first saw Bonnard's paintings and revelled in their colour. He also met James Joyce and Ezra Pound through Wyndham Lewis. It was a fruitful trip.

Although the main reason for living in Chelsea was affordability, Dobson's studio was well-situated in terms of social networks. Sir Osbert Sitwell lived down the road, and besides Ben Nicholson, TE Lawrence (Lawrence of Arabia) was also a neighbour. Dobson began a portrait bust of Sitwell which took three months of daily sittings to complete. Lawrence was a regular visitor to Dobson's studio and would arrive silently, often while Osbert was posing. In fact, Lawrence was so impressed by Dobson's sculpture that he bought a cast of the finished head, which he first lent and then bequeathed to the Tate Gallery. He described it as follows: 'Appropriate, authentic and magnificent in my eyes, I think it's his finest piece of portraiture and in addition it's as loud as the massed band of the Guards.'

This magnificent polished bronze head of Osbert Sitwell (1922) is sometimes mistakenly identified as brass. It looks brassy because it has no patina to colour it, and both bronze and brass are copper alloys. (Bronze consists of copper and tin whereas brass is a mixture of copper and zinc.) The highly polished finish was eminently suitable for such a sophisticated sitter, while the visual echo of Brancusi's gleaming forms in its presentation and use of materials offered a nice Post-Impressionist touch, and jazzy surface reflections made it even more contemporary.

There is an amusing coda to the story of this portrait, as recorded in Sitwell's memoirs. Two years after TE Lawrence first lent the bronze head to the Tate, Osbert, on a visit to the gallery, was startled by a salute from the man on the entrance turnstile. This official, noticing his surprise, responded: 'Bless my soul, sir, we're old friends. Scrubs your head every Wednesday, I do!'

In 1924 Dobson was chosen to represent the sculpture of Great Britain at the Venice Biennale with the late Gaudier-Brzeska, and won all sorts of acclaim in the process. He was also able to visit Italy for the first time, staying in Portofino, then travelling round the country and ending up in Venice. He visited the Medici Chapels in

Sir Osbert Sitwell, polished bronze, 2022, ed 3, estate stamp, h 32 cm
Cast from the 1922 plaster

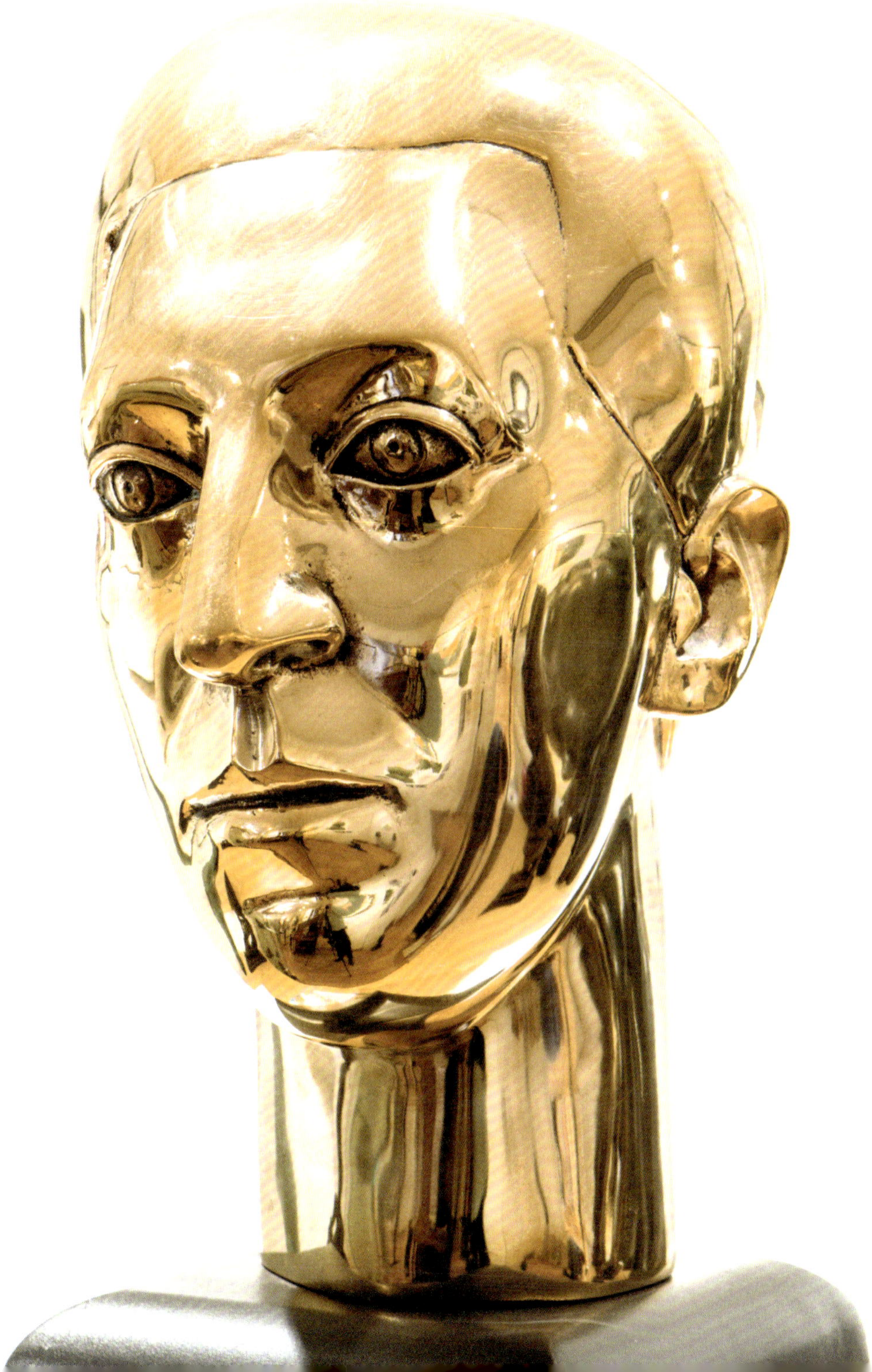

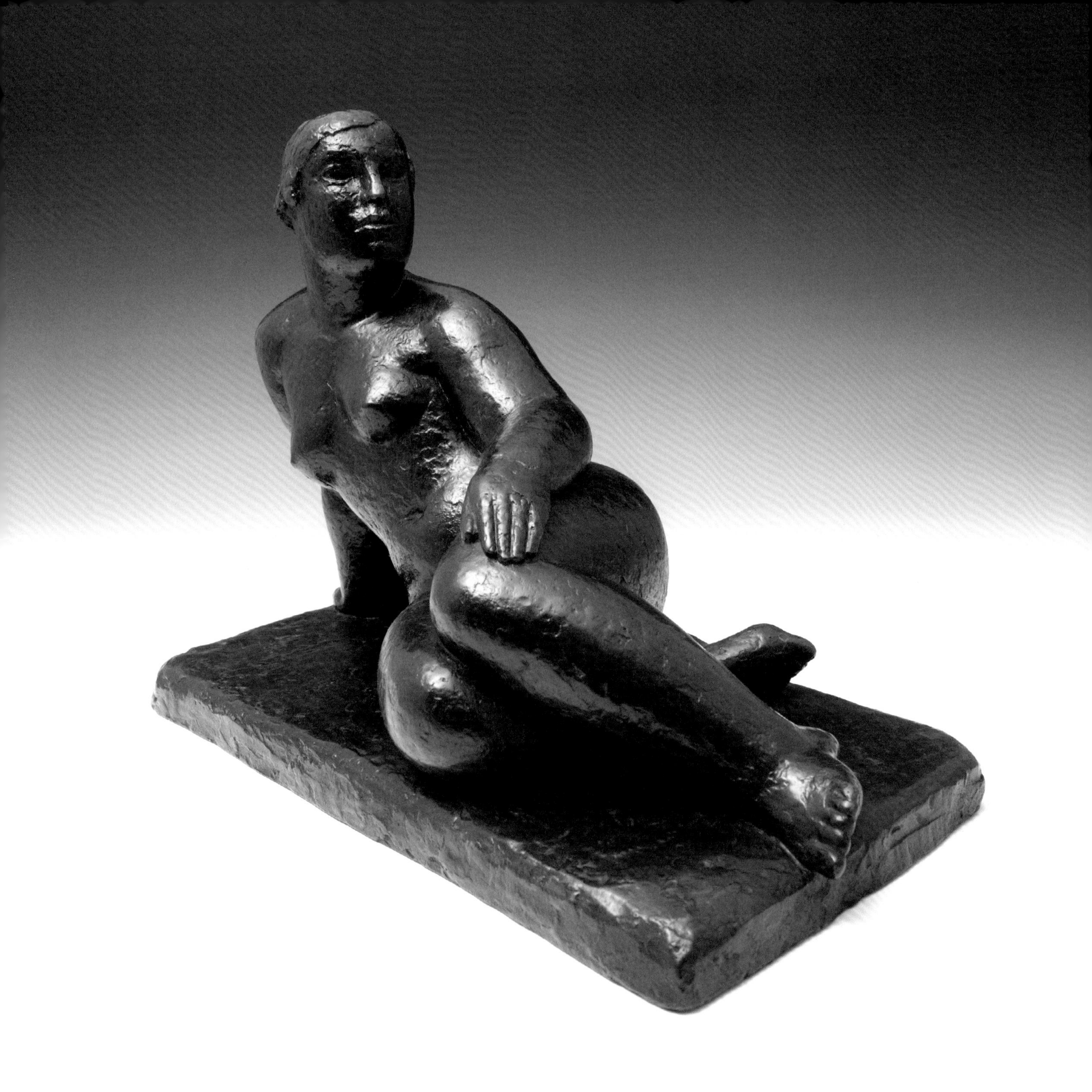

Florence and saw Michelangelo's great single reclining figures: *Day* and *Night*, *Dawn* and *Dusk*. He was much impressed by these which were to exert an abiding influence over his work.

1925 was another year of important travel, with Dobson being offered the chance of a trip to Ceylon with his wealthy patron and friend, the novelist Leo Myers. Dobson travelled in style with him, and stayed in some luxury, which must have been deeply appreciated by the often cash-strapped artist. The Ceylon trip was a great stimulus to him, informing the work he made on his return with a breath of the East.

For contemporary artists, there were various venues in which to exhibit work, and source a precarious income. Dobson showed with the Modern English Watercolour Society, for instance, in 1929, with the likes of John and Paul Nash, Epstein, Ben Nicholson and Leon Underwood. Then there was the The London Group. In the 1920s, the LG numbered among its members Roger Fry, Duncan Grant and Vanessa Bell, Mark Gertler and Matthew Smith, with Sickert, William Roberts and the Nash brothers contributing regularly. Dobson was elected a member in 1922 and then voted President, from 1924-26. There were other exhibiting bodies, and other income possibilities to explore, and in 1920s and 30s

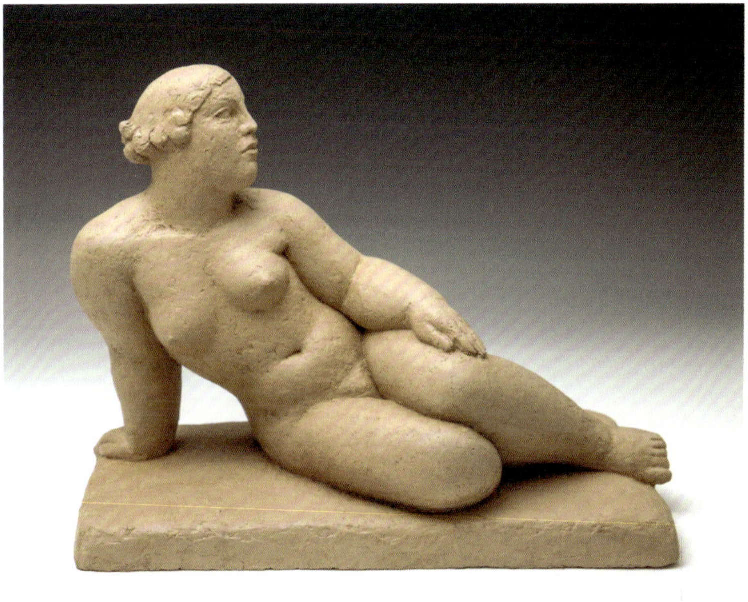

Dobson executed a number of fabric designs, maintaining his reputation for versatility.

Dobson had by now become good friends with Augustus John and they frequently attended the same parties and social gatherings, including those at the Cheyne Walk home Christopher Wood shared with Tony Gandarillas in the mid-1920s. It seems that Dobson, with his freedom of response, ready friendship and wide experience, was an important figure for younger artists.

Reclining Nude Figure, bronze, 2016, ed 12, signed, h 33 cm
The first cast from the 1928 terracotta
Reclining Nude Figure, terracotta, 1928, signed, h 33 cm

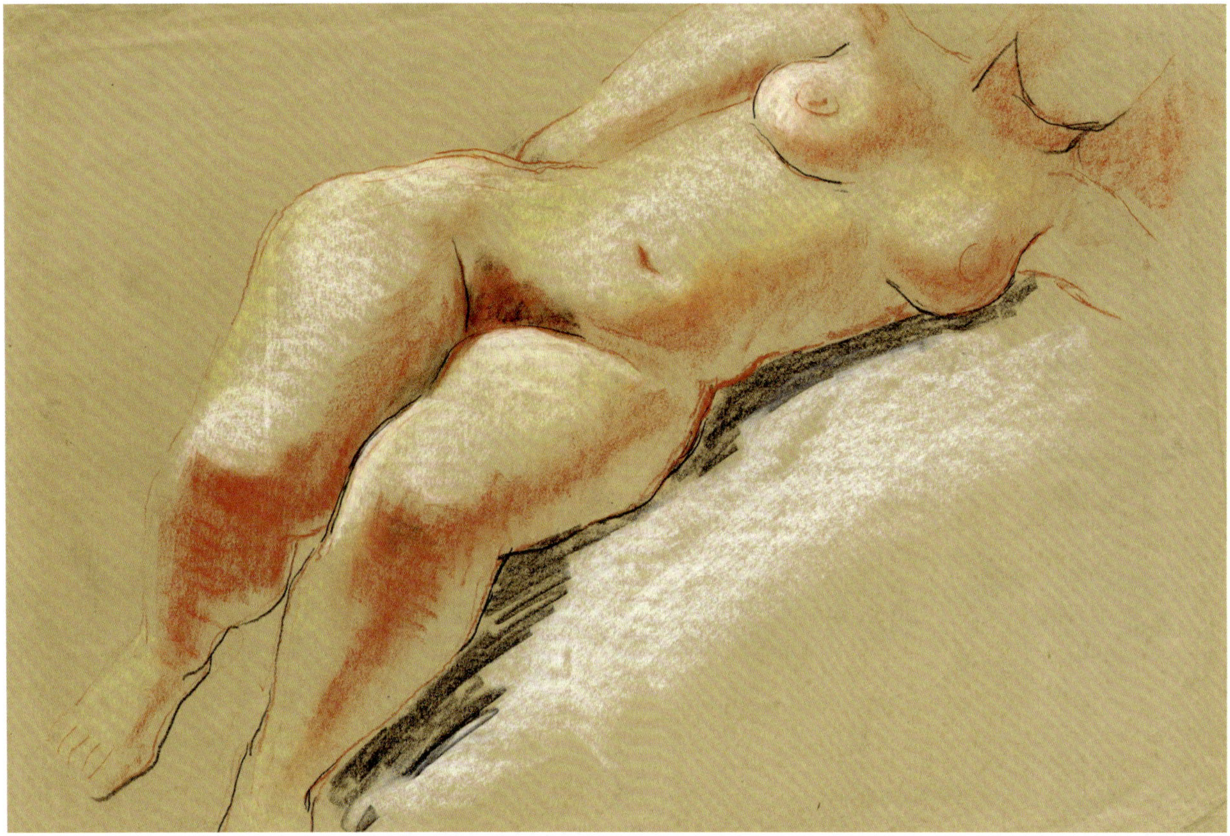

Besides Ben Nicholson he was also a formative influence on Christopher Wood, advising and encouraging him. Certainly, Dobson stayed with Wood in Paris in 1926, and the young painter wrote enthusiastically to his mother: 'Dobson, who has known Augustus John since he began, says I am the only person in England who has begun with as much talent and the same greatness in his mentality and work.' Dobson's encouragement was by way of a challenge — just the sort of fillip Wood then needed.

And it was in part Dobson's knowledge of Cornwall that inspired Wood to visit St Ives in 1926, which led to his and Ben Nicholson's

Reclining Nude, chalk, 38 x 56 cm

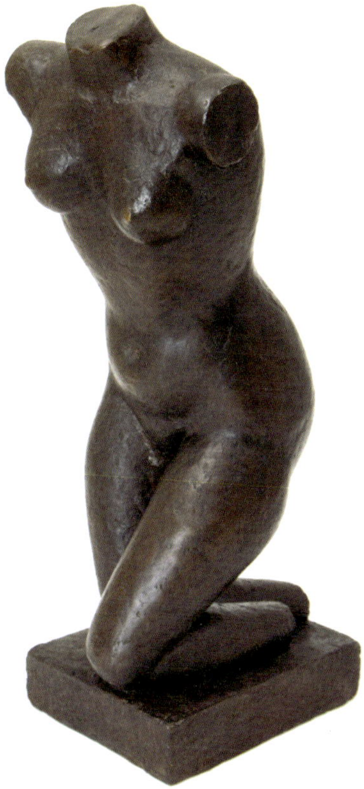

crucial discovery of Alfred Wallis there two years later. Meanwhile, John and Dobson carried on as friends and advisors to Wood. Eventually, the influence of Ben Nicholson and his wife Winifred was to outweigh Dobson's, and Wood and the Nicholsons became very close allies. It was also in 1926 that Dobson's second wife, Mary Bussell, came into his life, and in September they travelled together to the south of France, staying over in Paris for Christmas. While there, Dobson saw work by Derain and Matisse, African sculpture, visited Zadkine's and Maillol's studios, and was befriended by Man Ray.

A compactly sensual bronze dated c1926 and simply titled *Woman Seated* is a fine example of the work from this period. It seems to refer to the *First Portrait of Mary* of the same year, and if it is not actually a portrait of Dobson's new wife (the face is perhaps not quite oval enough), it is certainly close in feeling. The wing of hair dropping over the face is reminiscent of the magnificent watercolour portrait Dobson made of her that year.

A plaster from a couple of years later, *Reclining Nude Figure* (c1928), has now been cast in bronze and is all sleek lines and ready appeal. The *Kneeling Torso* bronze from 1928 is one of those balancing figures that Dobson was so fond of and made throughout his career — leaning towards or away from the viewer, showing the body as a living, moving entity, with its own changing dynamics, and not frozen in some awkward pose. The naturalness is compelling, and the skill in rendering flesh and muscle tone is deeply convincing.

Kneeling Torso, bronze, 2021, ed 12, signed, h 46 cm
Cast from the 1928 bronze

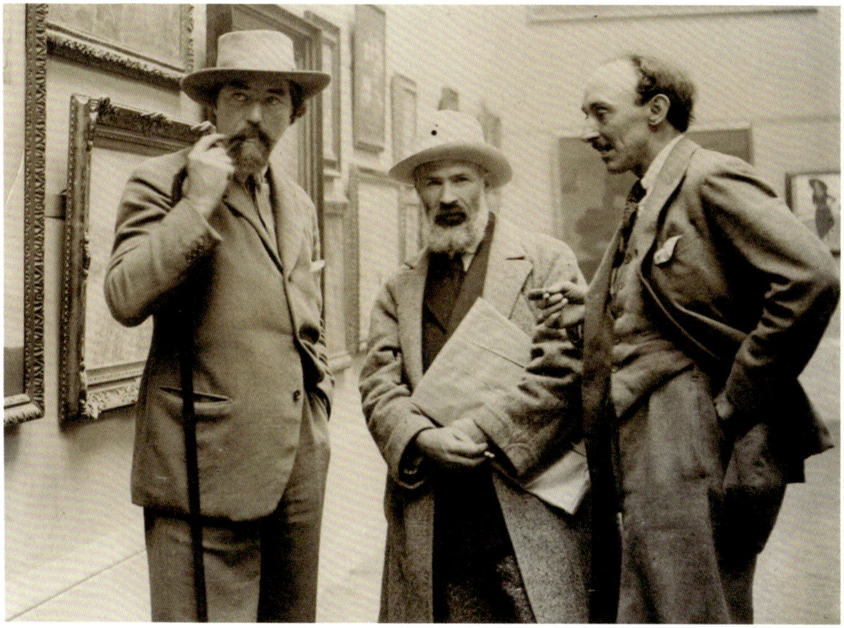

Augustus John, Constantin Brancusi, Frank Owen Dobson, by unknown photographer, circa 1925

Mary Dobson's sister May was married to T W (Tommy) Earp, the writer and critic, good friend and supporter of both Augustus John and Dobson, and back in England this group became even more tightly-knit. 1926 was turning into a year to remember, as Dobson again represented Britain at the Venice Biennale, and this time he and the critic PG Konody hung the exhibition. There's a marvellous and rather revealing photograph of Augustus John, Brancusi and Dobson standing together (c1925) in the midst of an exhibition somewhere, possibly even in Venice. The photo says much about the characters of all three protagonists. Typically, it is Brancusi who is centre stage and commands the limelight by glaring at the camera. John (apparently above such matters as having his photograph taken) glances absently off to the right, while Dobson looks modestly at Brancusi.

By all accounts, Frank Dobson was a congenial companion with room in his soul to admire the achievements of others. Perhaps he lacked the killer instinct that so many really successful artists are said to possess. A practical man, he valued application and good craftsmanship, and had little enthusiasm for art movements or theories. In March 1927, he held his second one-man exhibition at the Leicester Galleries, and it was this show that established him finally, at the age of 40, at the centre of the art world.

One of the most exciting recent discoveries for Dobson enthusiasts is a lost sculpture called *The Nest*. Not included in Neville Jason's complete catalogue of the sculpture, published in 1994, it came to Goldmark through customers who chanced upon it at auction. The identity of the sculpture was confirmed when Goldmark researchers discovered the existence of a Dobson drawing in the permanent collection of the V&A. Entitled *Study for Sculpture: a bird feeding nestlings*, it is done in black, white and brown chalks on pink-toned paper. The drawing is very close to the sculpture and is a clear confirmation of the authenticity of this work.

This must be one of Dobson's most abstract drawings, apart from his designs for textiles and furnishing fabrics. (Examples of these too are in the V&A.) The sculpture is similarly abstracted. The enclosing sphere of the bird's body protects the chicks, while its wings jut out threateningly like blades or rockets, to deter potential predators. In fact, from behind, the sculpture could almost be a gun turret, and this mechanistic aspect suggests comparison with the Vorticist art of Dobson's friend Wyndham Lewis. Hence the tentative dating of this piece to the 1920s. We can find no previous public record of *The Nest*, so now an edition has been cast and the image is published for the first time. This represents a distinct coup for Goldmark Gallery and for the Dobson Estate.

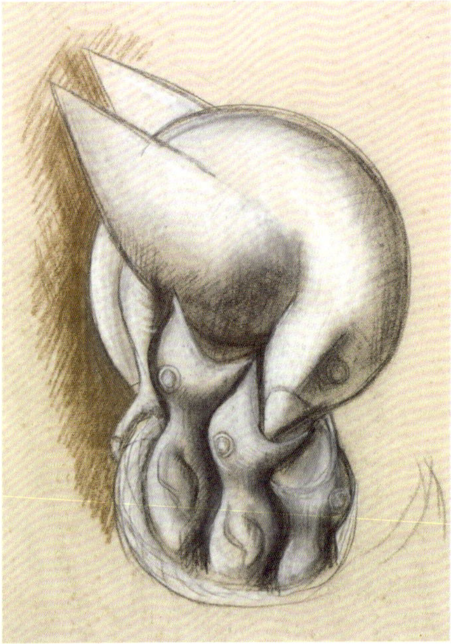

Study for Sculpture: a bird feeding nestlings, coloured chalk, 38.7 x 29.2 cm

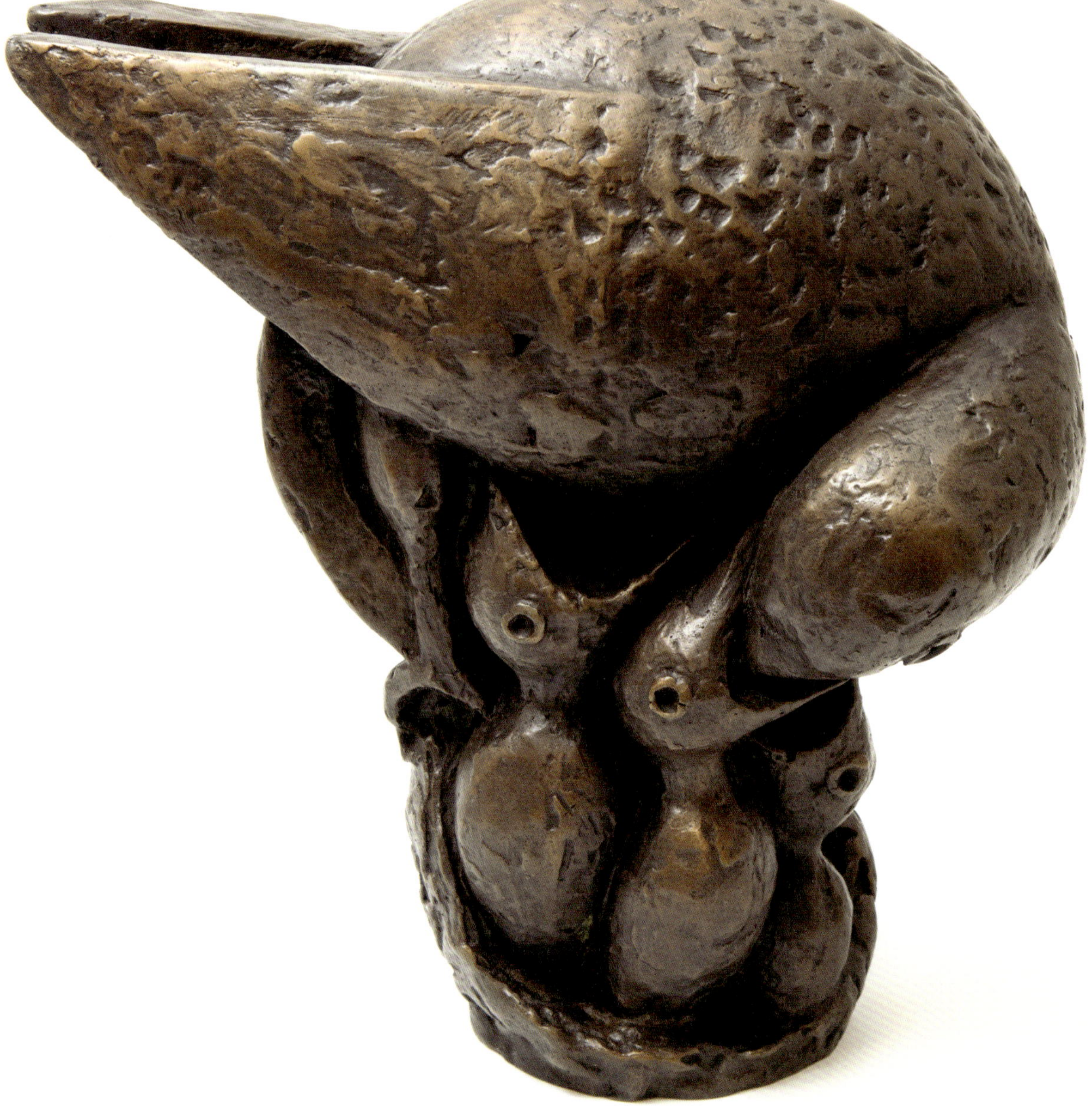

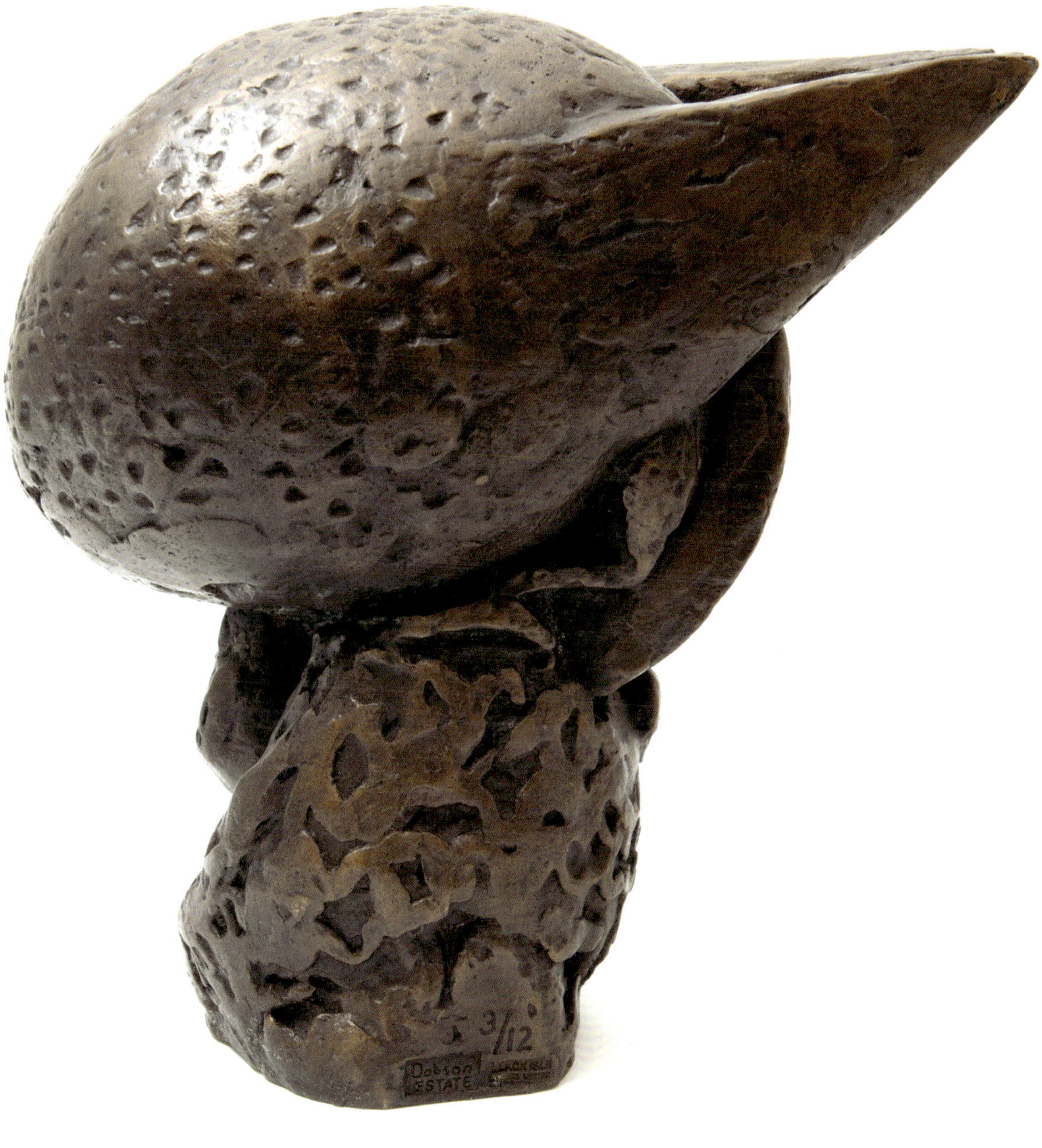

The Nest, (front and rear), bronze, 2020, ed 12, estate stamp, h 34 cm
The first casting from plaster of this piece believed to have been modelled sometime in the 1930s

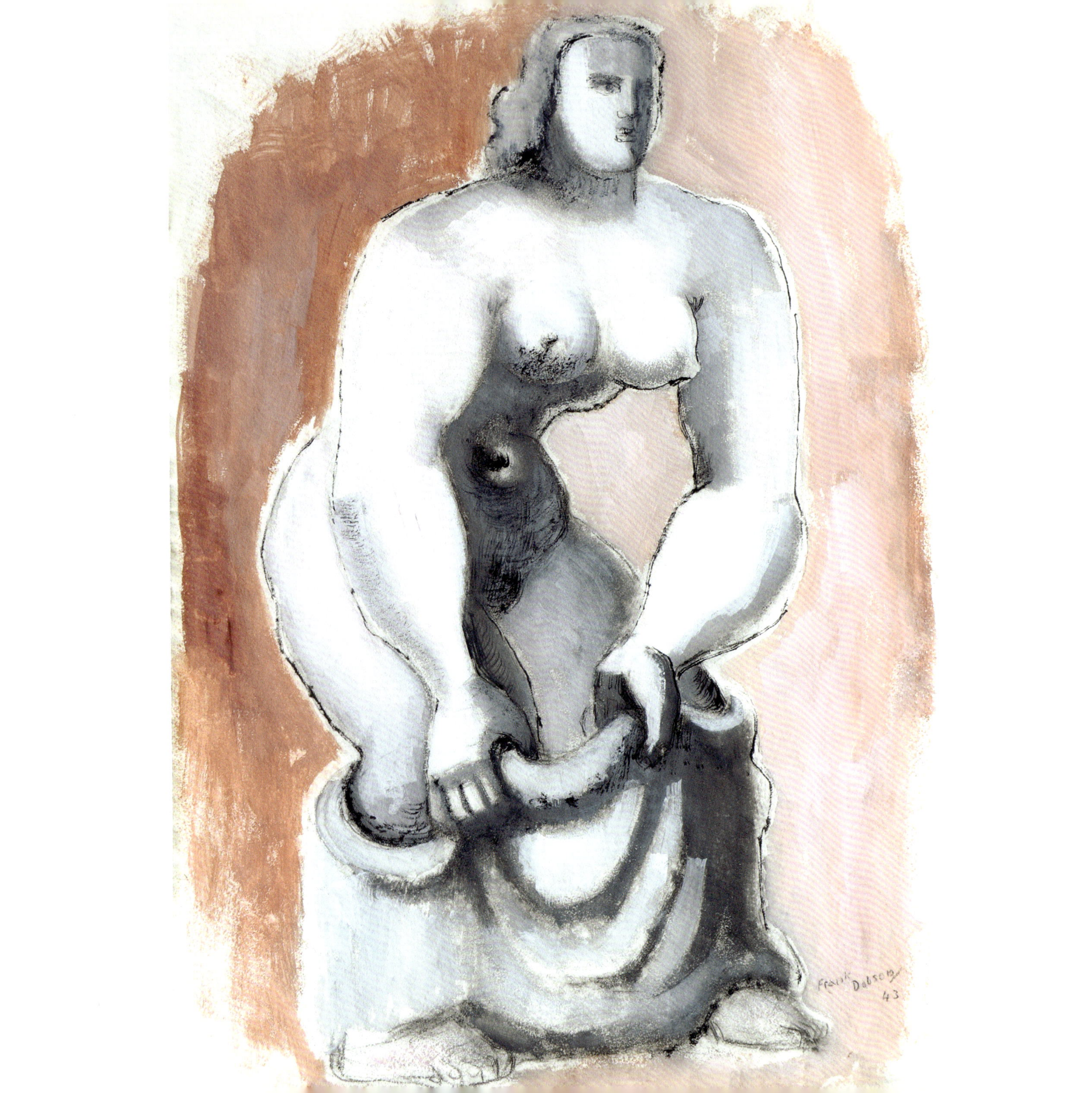
Frank Dobson
43

4

The 1930s and War Again (1930-45)

Woman with Towel, pencil, watercolour & gouache, 1943, signed, 57 x 39 cm

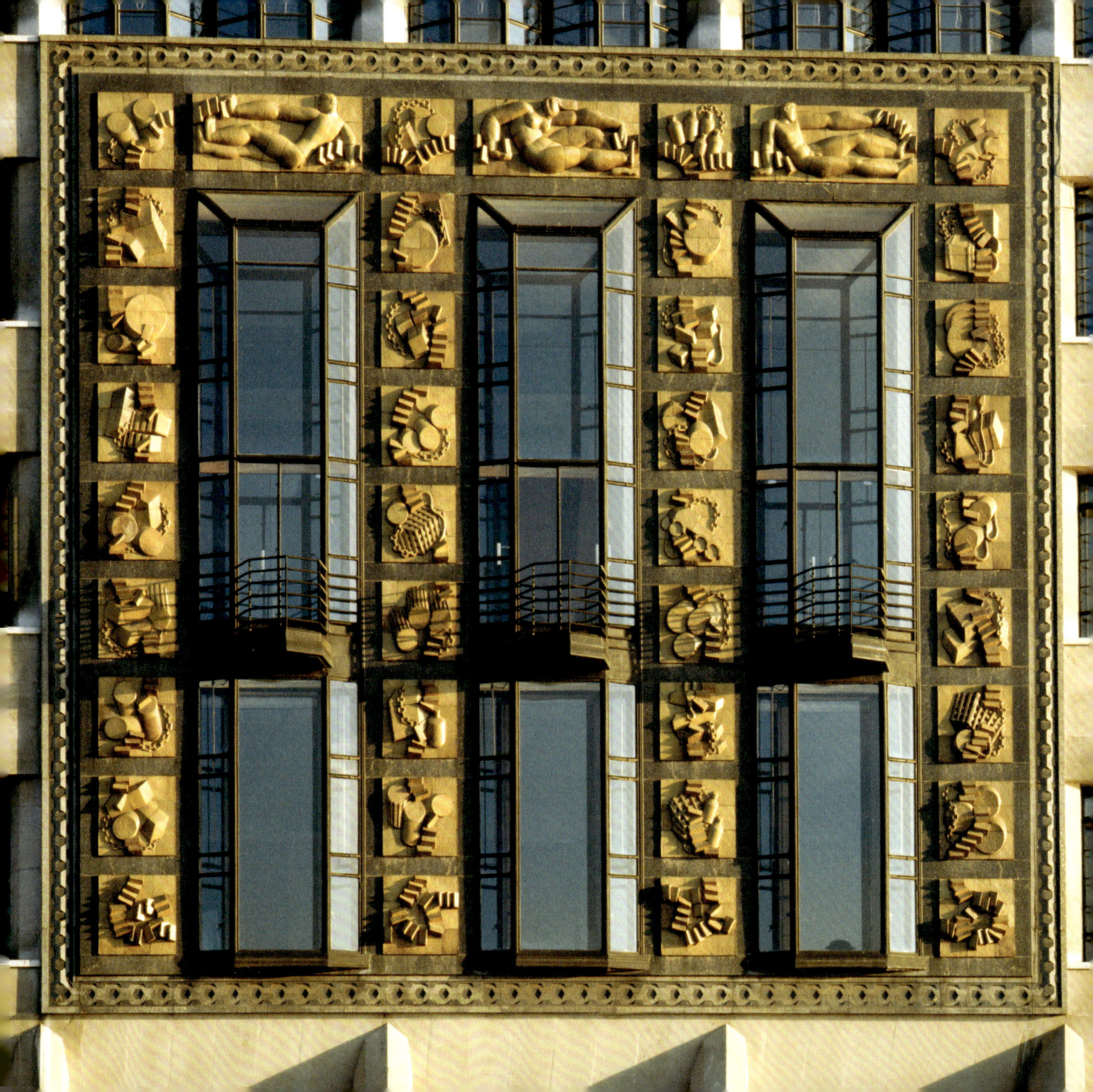

'If you want a mere record, what's wrong with a Kodak?'

Frank Dobson

The decade of the 1930s opened with a major architectural commission for Dobson to supply relief panels for the riverside exterior of HS Goodhart-Rendel's Hays Wharf building on the Thames. Dobson thought of this as essentially decorative work rather than true sculpture, and the gilded faience in which he worked does indeed make a strikingly ornate and memorable contrast with the black granite setting of the trio of tall windows. The theme is commerce, capital and labour, and Dobson has for once constructed a visual narrative: a bold decorative device of scrolling logs or steps holding the individual scenes together, linking then like a ribbon. Four vertical columns articulate the facade with a horizontal screen at the top, depicting massive figures at rest: it is an impressive achievement and still recognisably Dobson's work.

The response to this commission was varied. The rather staid painter Randolph Schwabe mentions visiting Hays Wharf in June 1932 and enjoying the liveliness of the decorations, but thought it 'more like a cocktail bar or a night-club than a warehouse'. Paul Nash, however, praised Dobson's faience work in *The Listener*, 16th March 1932. In the economically depressed Thirties artists were always looking for new ways of generating income, and working in the applied arts was good business. The highly articulate

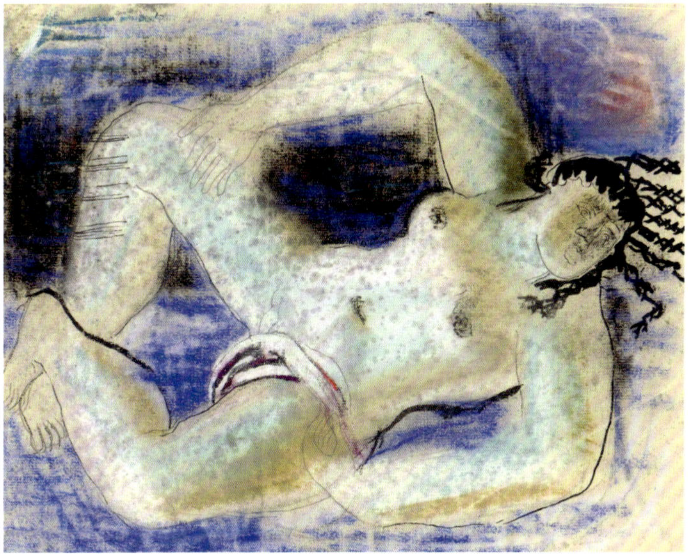

Hay's Wharf, London, relief panels by Frank Dobson, © Angelo Hornak / Alamy
Recumbent Nude, chalk & ink, 31 x 25.5 cm

Nash took to writing as well. This was at a time when he was President of the Society of Industrial Artists (1932-5), and Dobson was on its council along with Graham Sutherland and the architect Serge Chermayeff.

Dealers were quick to take note of Dobson's increasing renown. In a mixed exhibition of contemporary drawings and sculptures mounted by the Zwemmer Gallery in November 1930, most of the drawings were by Gaudier, the others divided between Epstein, Dobson and Moore. Of the six sculptures included, four were by Gaudier and the other two by Dobson. The implication was clear: Dobson was Gaudier's successor. This was reinforced by the prices of the drawings: the Gaudiers ranged between 8 and 18 guineas, all seven of Dobson's were 18 guineas each, and while the elder statesman Epstein's were 21 guineas each, Moore's were offered at between 9 and 15 guineas.

Rhoda, a unique bronze from 1930, with distinctive green patina, shows what Dobson could do as a portraitist. The strong columnar neck is the stalk upon which the sensitively sculpted features sit. The tilt of the head expresses character in no uncertain terms. More deliberately beguiling is *Standing Torso* of five years later, a unique terracotta now editioned in bronze with a blue-green patina suggesting the sea. Subtitled *Study for Persephone 3*, it makes a splendid contrast to *Study for Persephone 1* of the same year, a five inch high unique headless terracotta, with the authenticity of an Attic figurine discovered in fishermen's nets off the coast of Rhodes.

But not everything was going Dobson's way, even in these high years of his acclaim. He was unlucky and slightly careless with his physical health, and particularly with his arms. (Compare

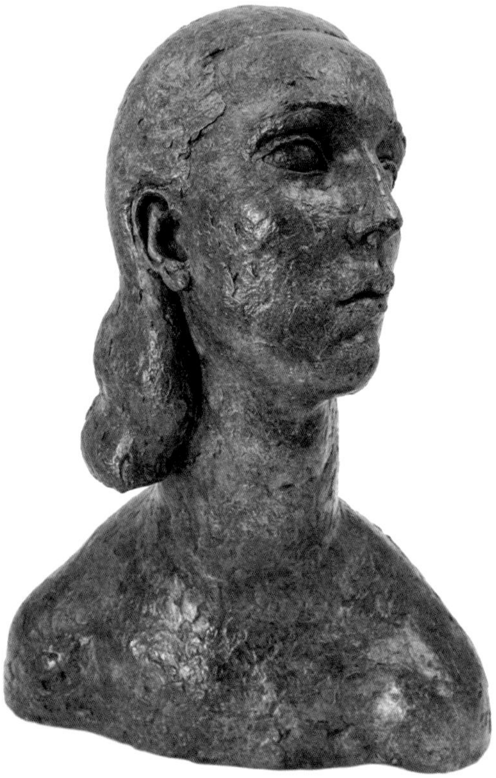

left & opposite: **Rhoda**, bronze, 2020, ed 12, estate stamp, h 51 cm
Cast from the unique 1930 bronze

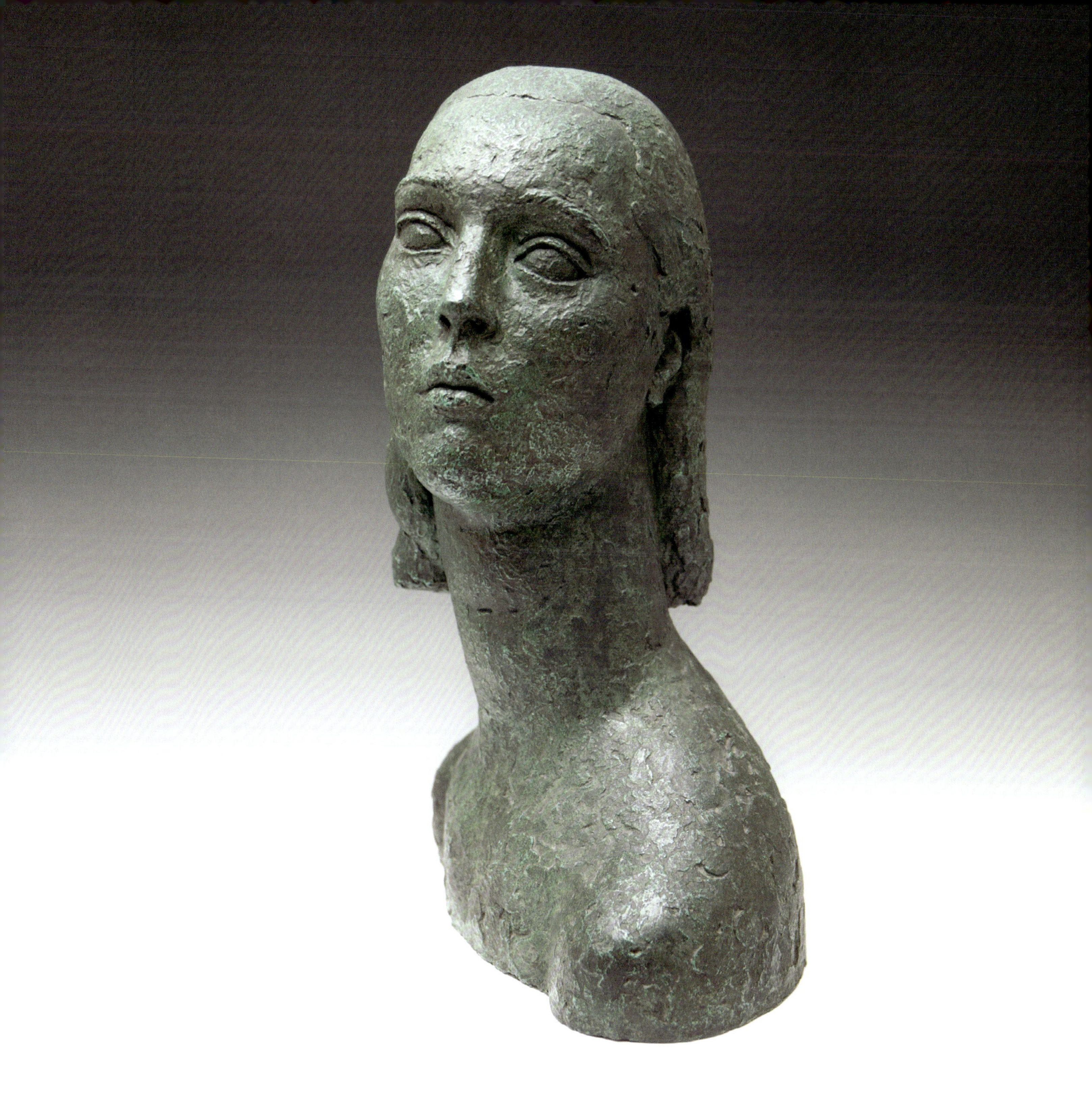

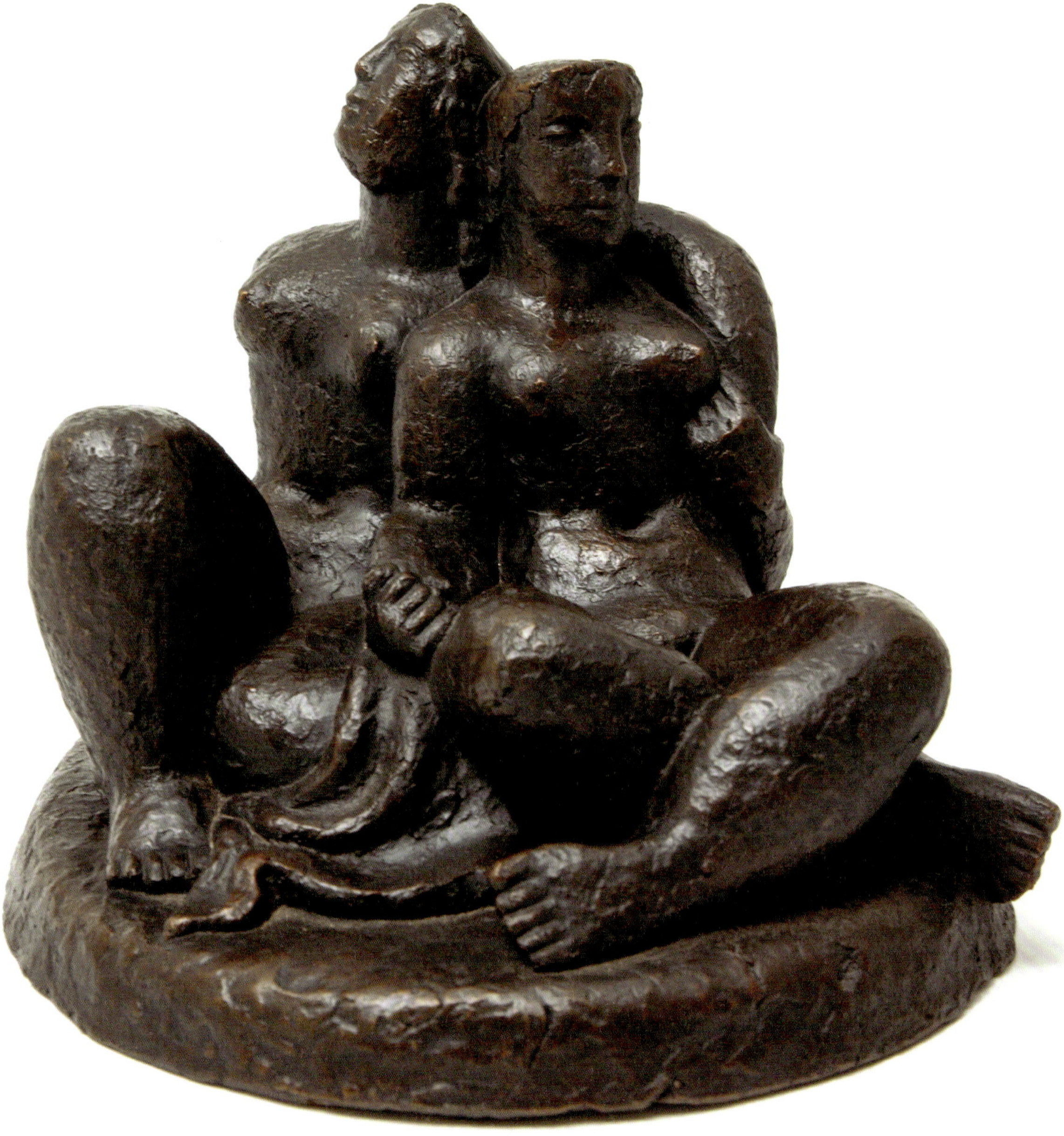

Dobson in this to Picasso, who was extremely protective of his hands and arms.) Dobson had the misfortune to break his left arm three times in his life, first in childhood. The third and final occasion was the worst. After a convivial drinking session in 1933, he raced a friend down Piccadilly, but slipped and fell, breaking his arm rather badly near the shoulder. Although this did not stop him carving as is sometimes alleged — he finished the magnificent *Pax* (1934), and continued working in stone into the 1950s (eg the marble *Reclining Female Figure* of 1954) — his output of carved sculpture did decrease.

More ideas were modelled in terracotta or plaster, and then either made into a small edition in that medium, or cast in bronze, usually in an equally small edition of three or four. In fact, many of the bronzes and terracottas remained unique. For example, *Noon* was originally modelled in terracotta in 1935-6, in an edition of three, one of which is in the Tate. It features two girls, intimate friends, perhaps lovers, but here in the grip of serenity rather than passion. This classical pagan figure group is substantial and grounded, very satisfying. The terracotta has now been cast in bronze in an edition of 10, fulfilling its sculptural potential and what was doubtless Dobson's original intention.

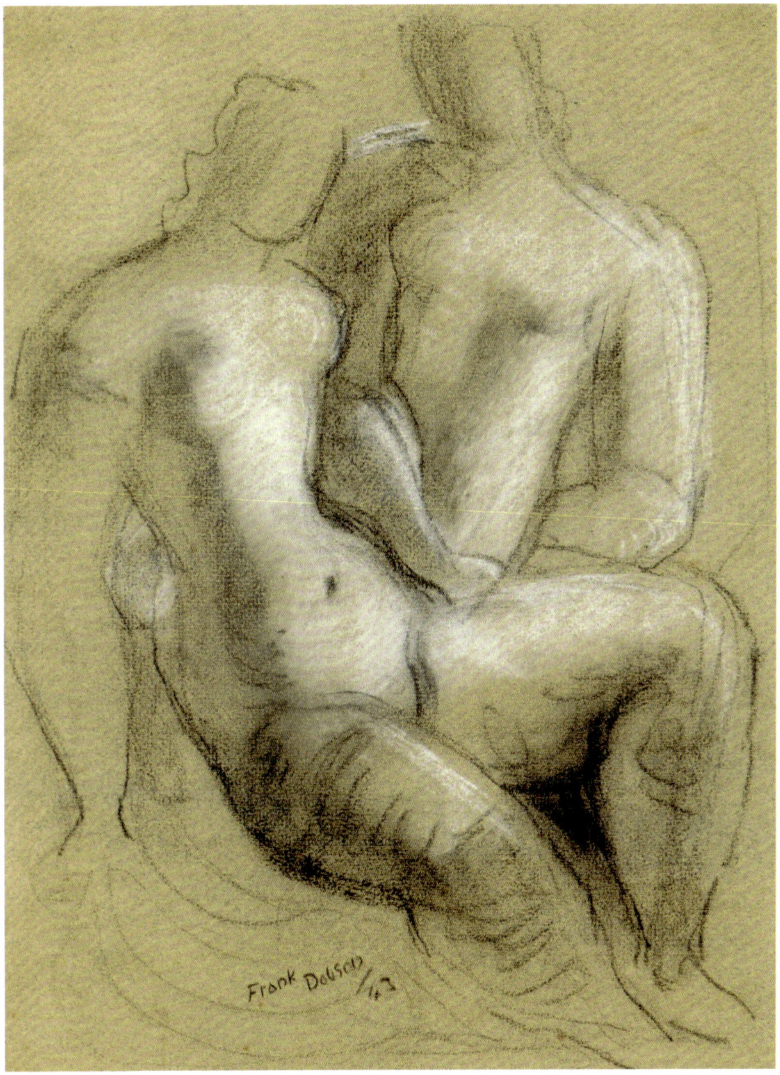

Noon, bronze, 2019, ed 10, signed, h 25 cm
Cast from the 1935-6 terracotta
Two Nudes, chalk, 1943, signed, 31.5 x 24 cm

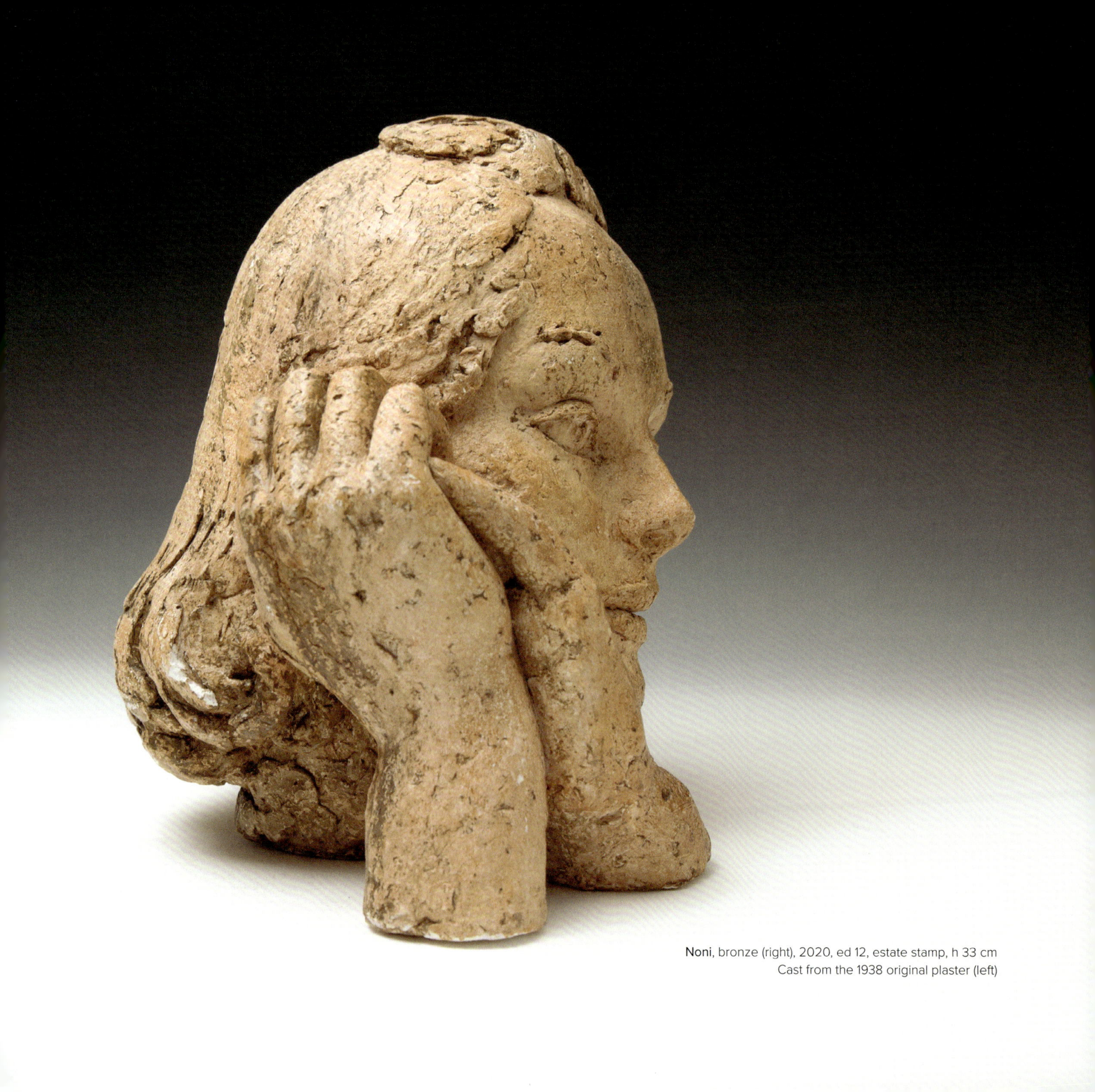

Noni, bronze (right), 2020, ed 12, estate stamp, h 33 cm
Cast from the 1938 original plaster (left)

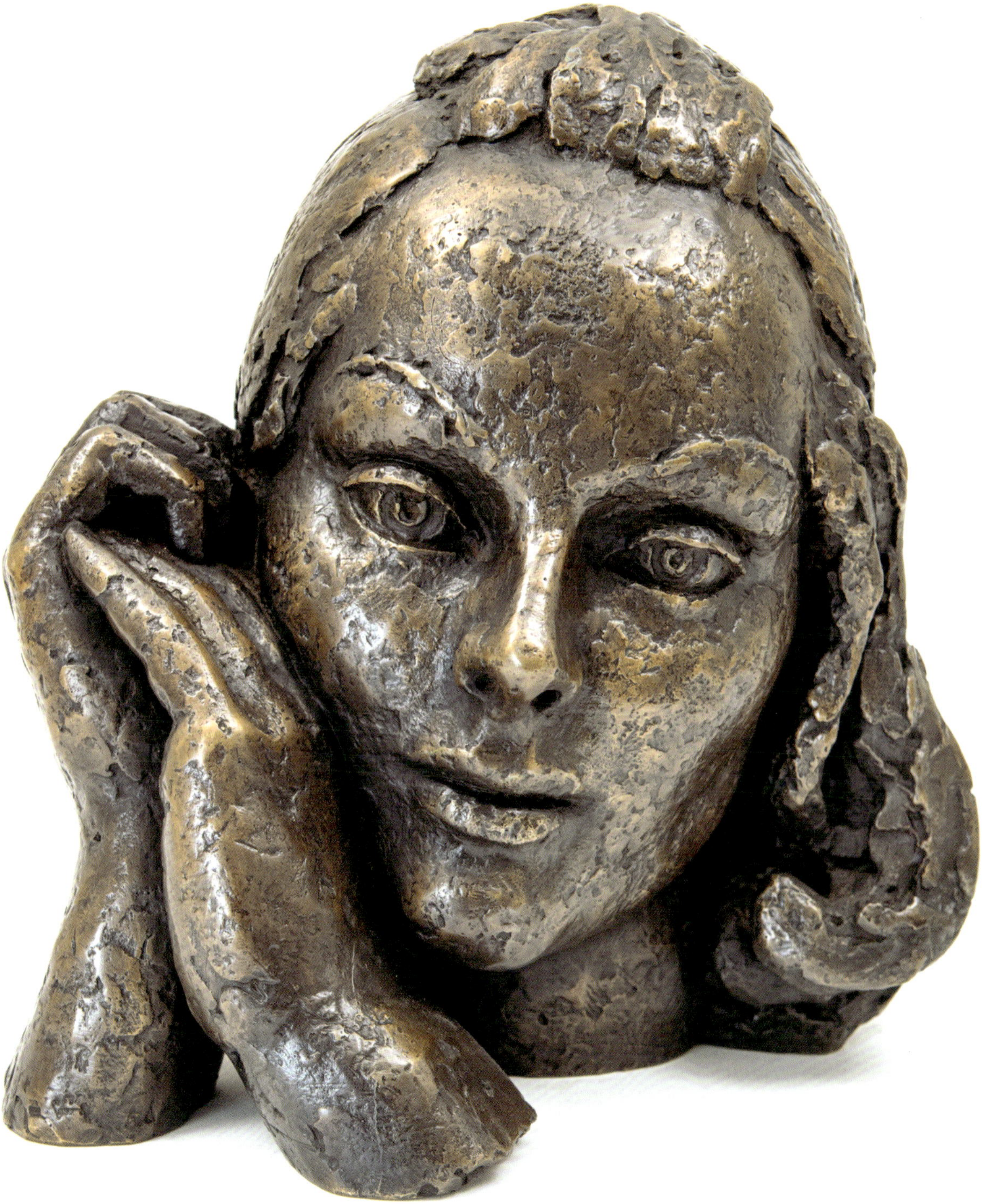

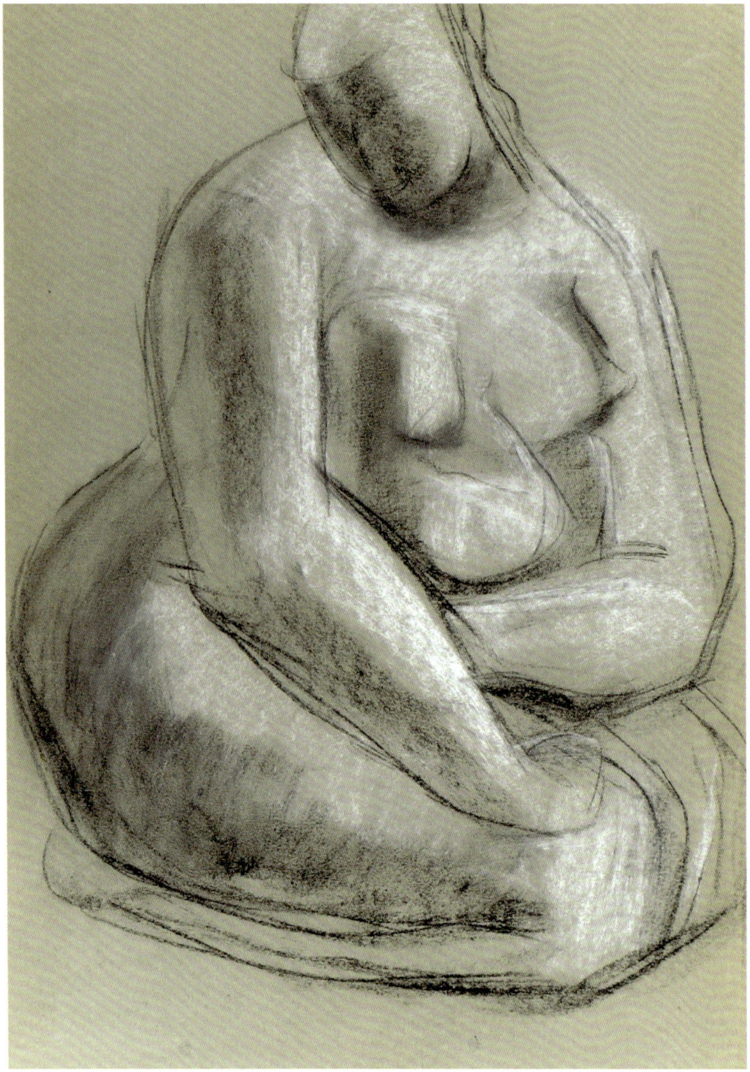

Another terracotta from this period, *Kneeling Figure* (1935), has a stalwart archaic look. This girl has seen it all, and remains unaffected; she is amoral rather than immoral, and decidedly more self-sufficient than the girls in *Noon*. She was made in an edition of four, of which one remains with the Estate. *Noni*, an original plaster from 1938, describes a girl with her hands together supporting her right cheek. This is a portrait of Joyce Adderbrook, a dancer with the famous Windmill Theatre ('We never close'), in the 1930s.

In August 1938 Dobson visited Maillol in France for the last time before war once again disrupted everyone's lives and Dobson's in particular: he was to have been the sole sculptor representing Britain at the Venice Biennale in 1940, but the exhibition was cancelled because of escalating hostilities. Even for an artist of Dobson's standing, earning money remained a major preoccupation and source of anxiety. With the outbreak of war, and being too old to fight, he naturally looked for work as a war artist. 'Saw a new drawing by Frank Dobson, of a fire in Bristol, very lurid & dramatic', wrote Randolph Schwabe in his journal, January 1941. But there was to be no regular employment for Dobson as a war artist. As he commented resignedly: 'I don't seem to have much luck with official work'.

Mother and Child, charcoal & chalk, 51 x 38 cm
Kneeling Figure, bronze, 2020, ed 12, estate stamp, h 22 cm
Cast from the 1935 terracotta

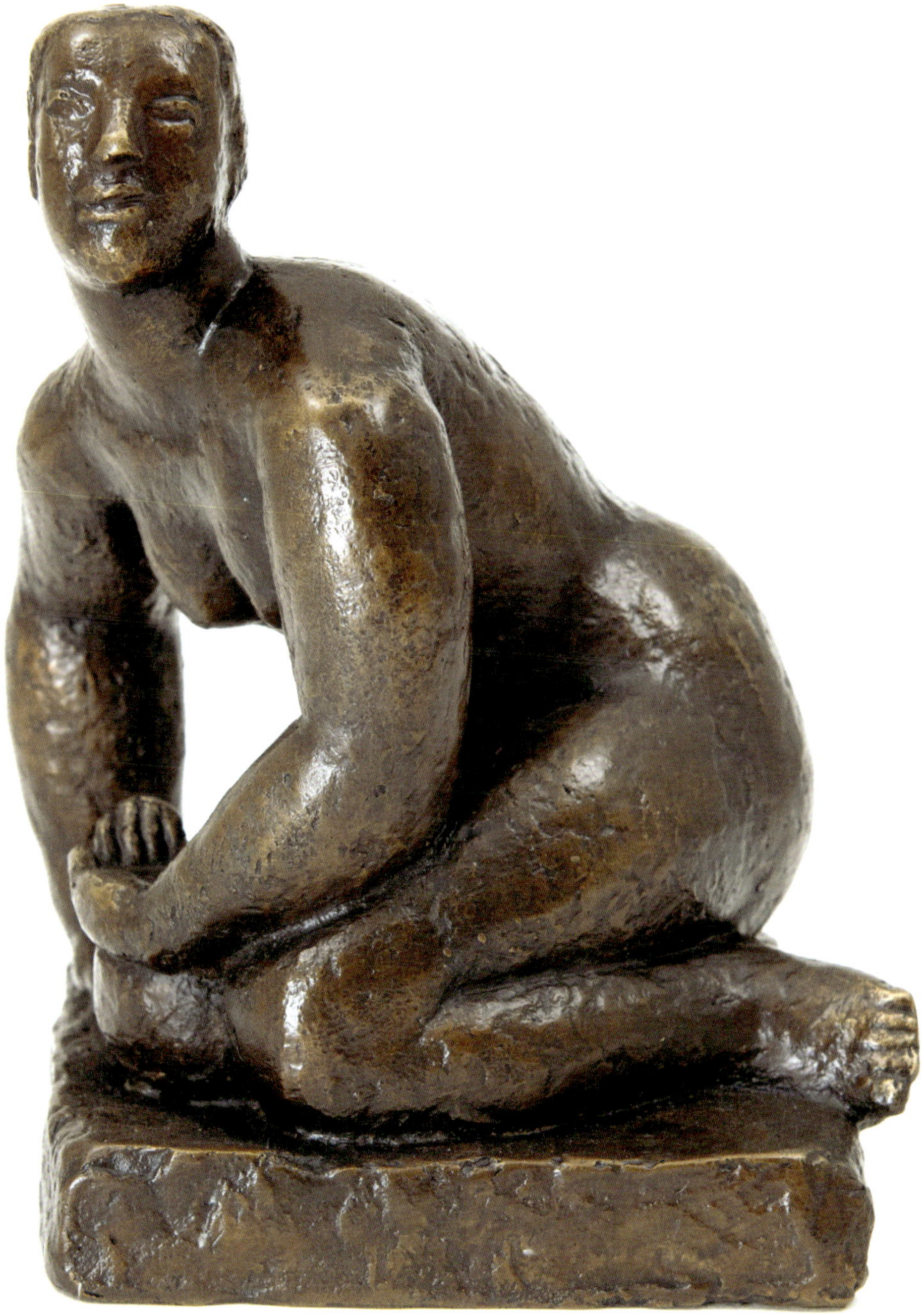

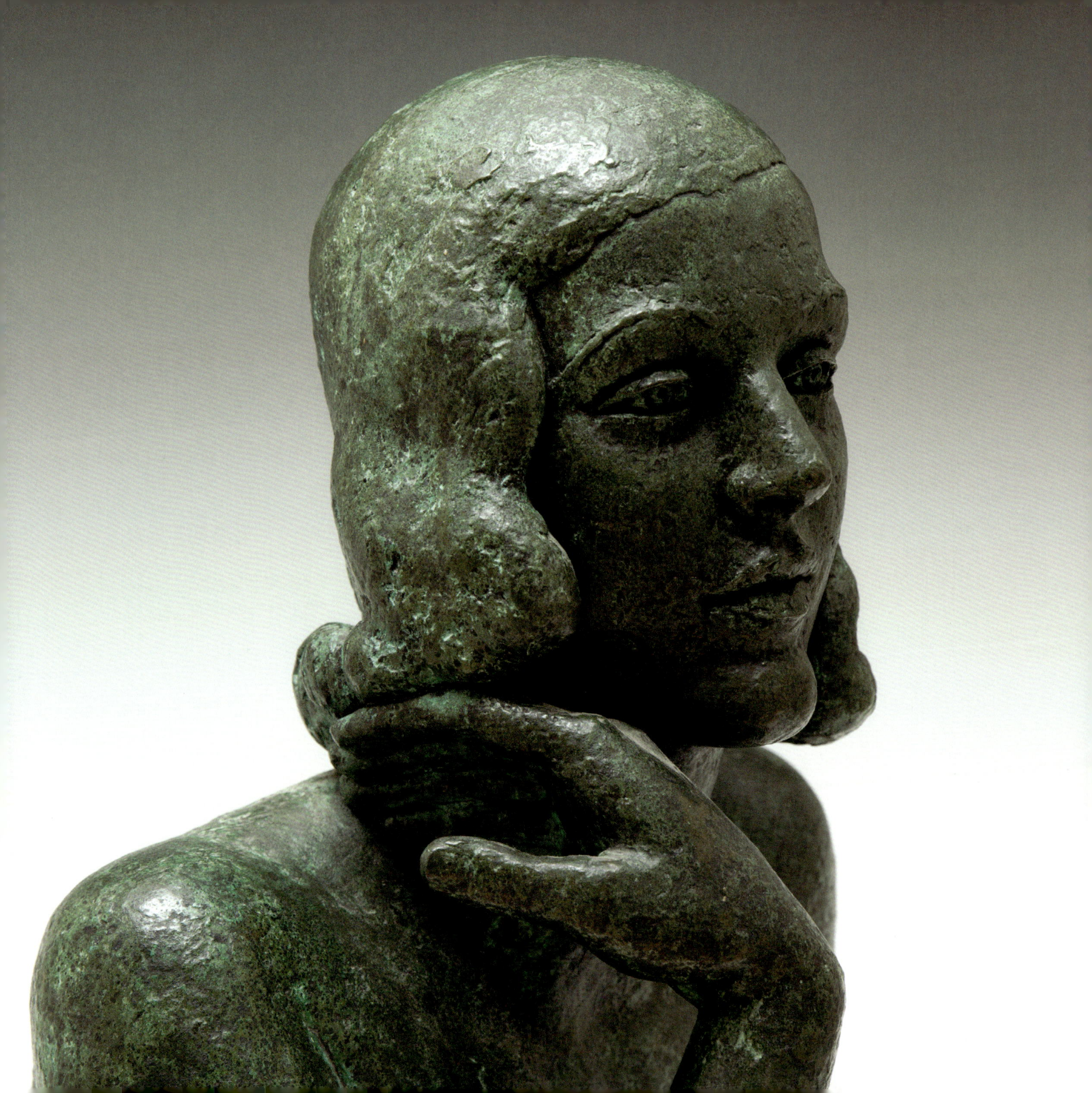

goldmark

October 2022

Sculpture, Drawings and Pots

Frank Dobson: 'Bring it Alive'

Our highly anticipated Frank Dobson show opening this month, featuring many never before editioned bronzes and some of Dobson's finest drawings and paintings, will also see the launch of our latest book: *Frank Dobson: 'Bring it Alive'*, penned by esteemed writer and critic Andrew Lambirth. 'There is a fundamental and unquenchable optimism to his work' writes Lambirth, 'which is primarily about pleasure and contentment and beauty... but always in the search for truth.' Dobson's friend, the artist Duncan Grant, went one further: 'I would call him a great sculptor; certainly one of England's greatest.'

Lisa Hammond, November 12th

Our sixth exhibition of pots by Britain's busiest potter, Lisa Hammond MBE, opens Saturday 12th November. Joining Lisa's internationally acclaimed repertoire of generous tsubo jars, rounded 'horse eye' bottles and her famed leaning jugs are a number of recent experiments: hand-carved kurinuki teabowls and work in a new black clay. Those featured in the show represent the finest pots Lisa has produced over the last three years, specially stashed away for this latest Goldmark exhibition.

Mike

Goldmark, Orange Street, Uppingham, Rutland, LE15 9SQ

01572 821424 www.goldmarkart.com

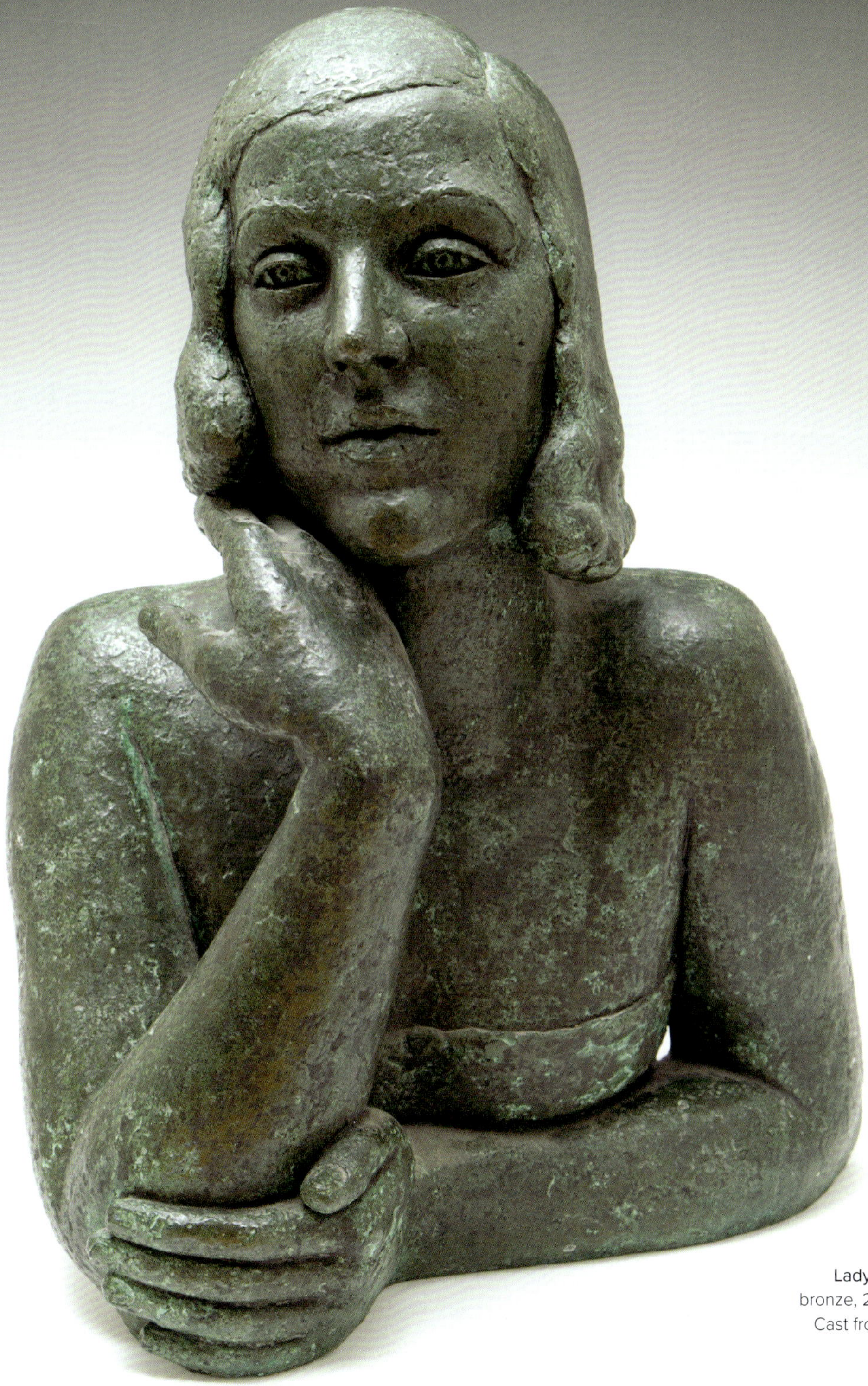

Lady Dorothea Ashley Cooper,
bronze, 2019, ed 9, signed, h 66 cm
Cast from the unique 1933 bronze

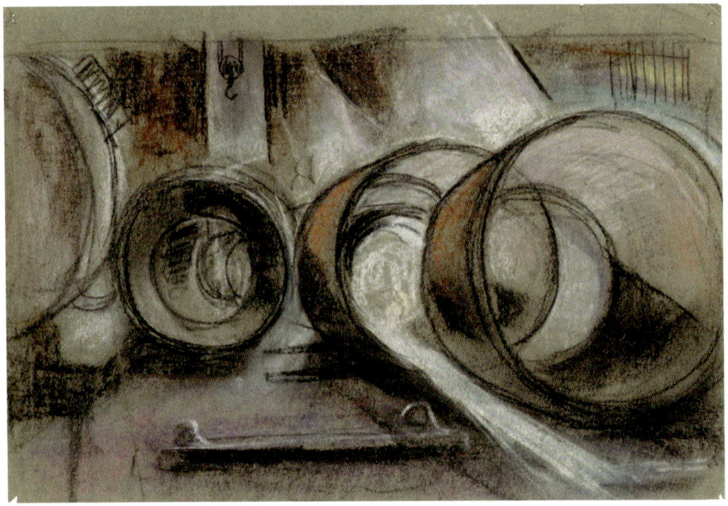

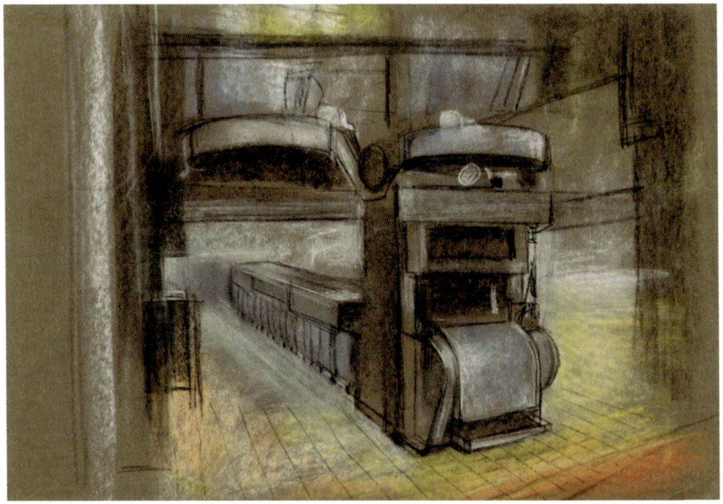

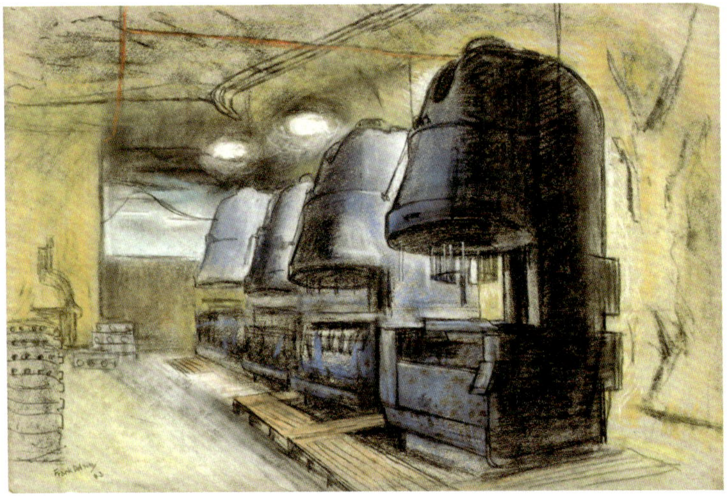

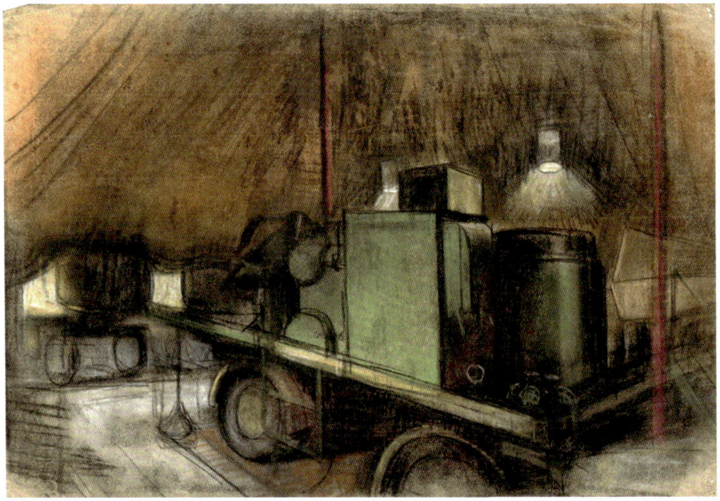

Tube Interiors III, chalk, 19 x 28 cm
The Belt, chalk, 38 x 56 cm
Jigsaws, chalk, 1943, signed, 32 x 48 cm
Machinery, chalk, 32 x 48 cm

Dobson was interested in new technology, and when the opportunity arose to record some of the industrial side of the war effort, he welcomed it. Sadly he was only given a short term contract by the War Artists' Advisory Committee, so he never became an official War Artist, though his work was purchased for the national collections. His bronze busts of Chief Petty Officer H J Whitehorne DSM and Admiral Sir William Millbourne James KCB (both 1941) were commissioned by the War Artists Advisory Committee for the Admiralty, and are now in the Imperial War Museum (IWM). From examples of his works on paper in the IWM, it's clear that Dobson tended to submit finished work in ink and watercolour or gouache, worked up in the studio from chalk drawings done on the spot. A number of these chalk studies remain in the Estate and are now exhibited for the first time.

Although one or two of these drawings bear a slight resemblance to the communications stations in the 1943 watercolour *An Underground Room in the BBC Building*, in the IWM, they are more likely to be on industrial themes. (Incidentally, Dobson proposed further BBC subjects but his ideas were rejected.) The forms of the machinery suggest condensers, multiple drills, marine boilers, a furnace, different types of

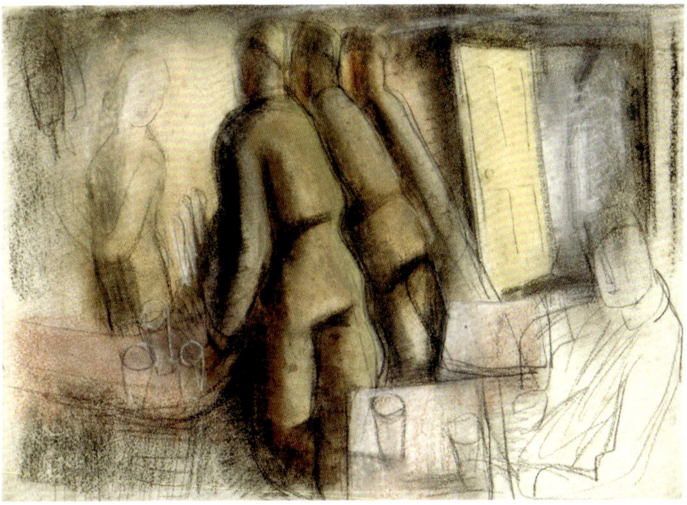

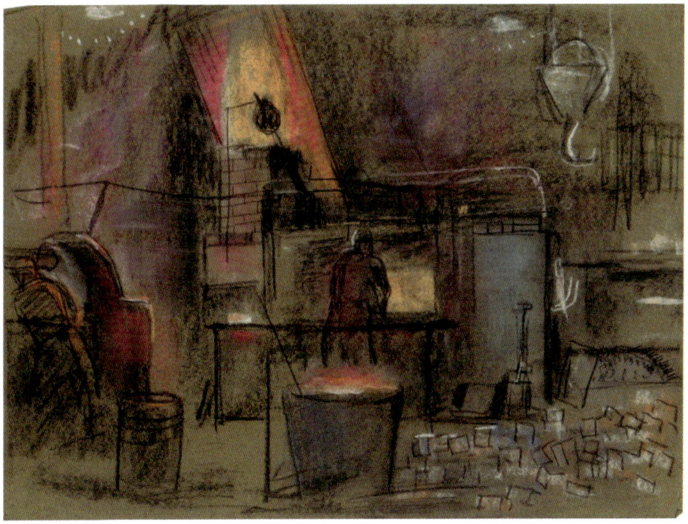

At the Bar, chalk & charcoal, 25.5 x 35.5 cm
At the Furnace, chalk, 28 x 38 cm

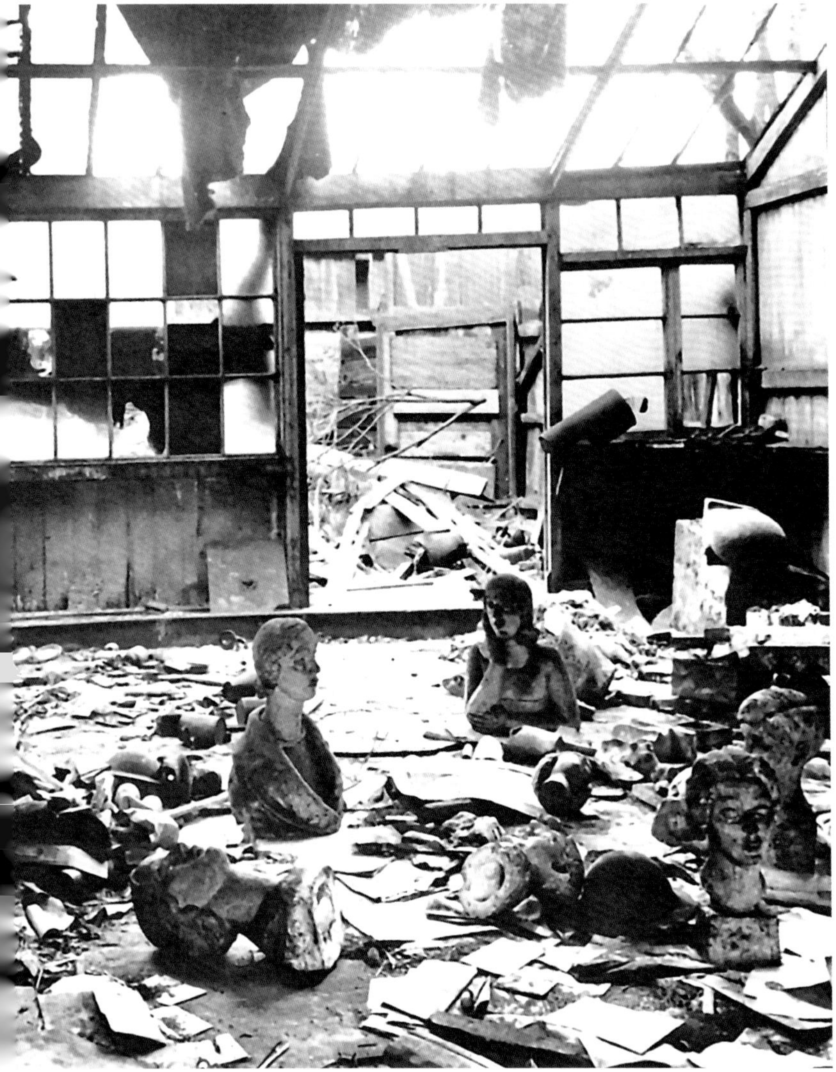

production line equipment, perhaps to do with munitions. The shapes on the page, their sculptural forms, are what carry these powerful images, and their subjects (pipe-laying? factory interiors? dockyards?) are secondary to the forms that have caught Dobson's interest. Perhaps this was why he was not used more as a war artist: his work was not thought documentary enough.

However, a larger ink and watercolour drawing of naval ratings clustering around a ship's gun (presumably for the purposes of instruction), does seem to be a companion piece to *Destroyer in Dry Dock*, a 1941 Dobson watercolour in the IWM collection. (Dobson here uses the same style of gouache painting — an ink armature filled out with bright colour, mostly vivid blues and mauves and pinks.) The subjects are clearly related and the use of a striking and very particular shade of blue is common to both. There is also a chalk study of three soldiers standing at a bar, ordering beer from the barmaid, while a fourth sits at a table in the right foreground. All four men wear forage caps. Compare this study to the watercolour and ink drawing in the IWM entitled *Four Soldiers Seated at a Table*, 1942. The IWM drawing could depict the very next moment, when the men, having collected their beer from the bar, sit down to drink.

Frank Dobson's bomb-damaged studio. Photographer unknown
Naval Gunners, watercolour, gouache & ink, 44 x 56 cm

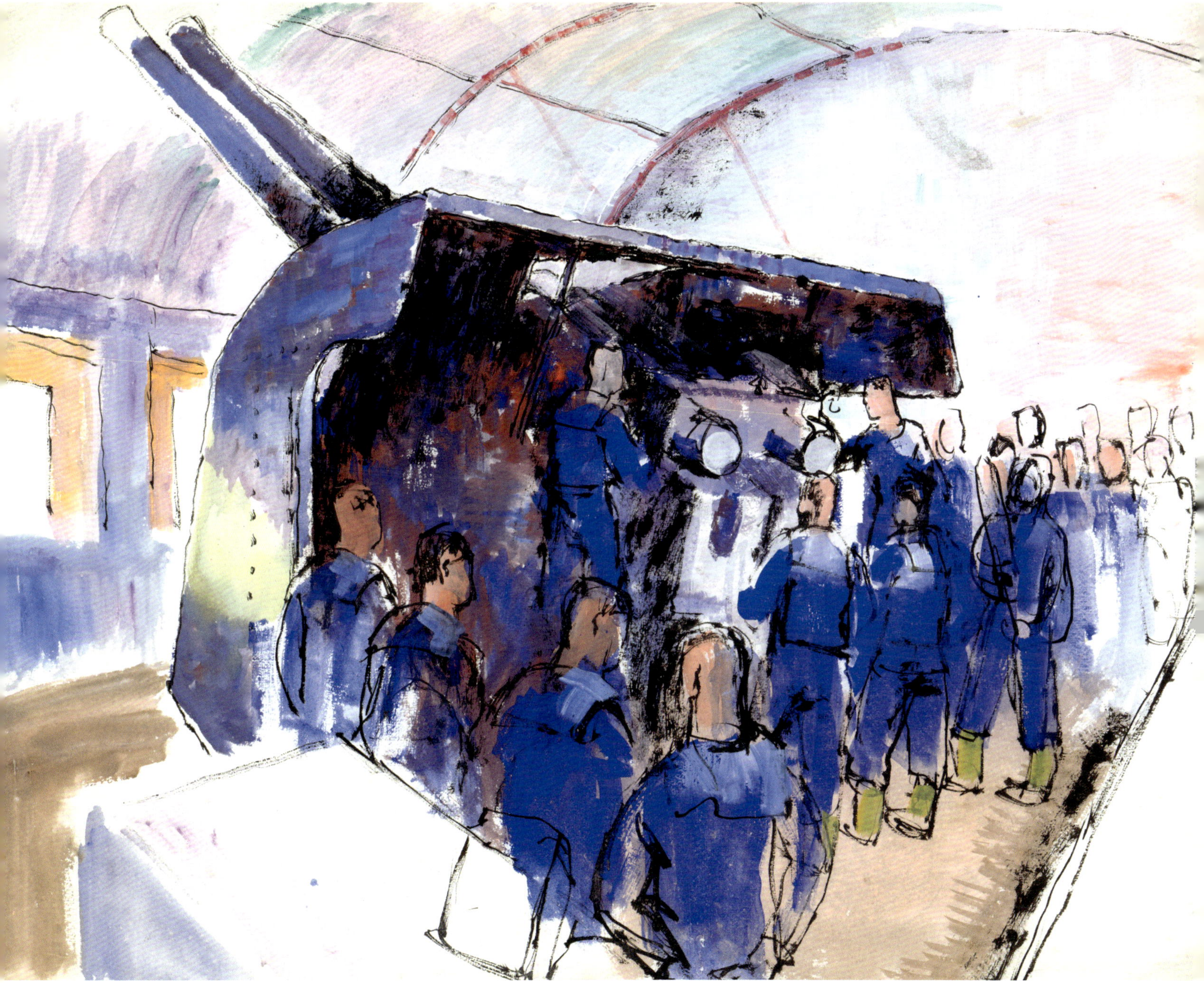

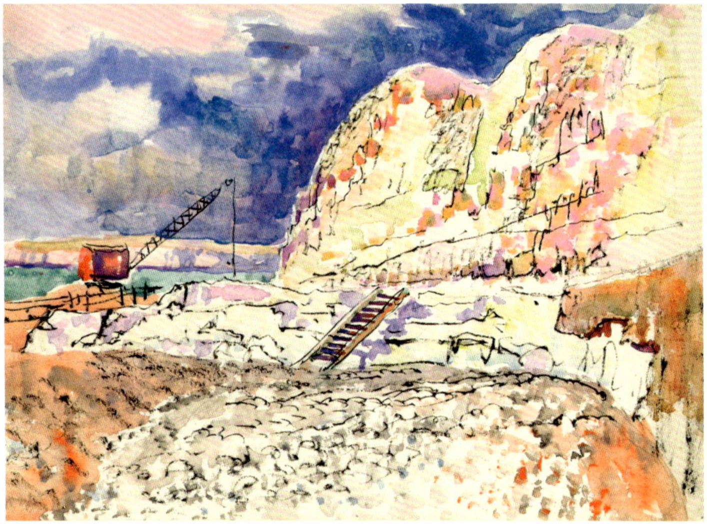

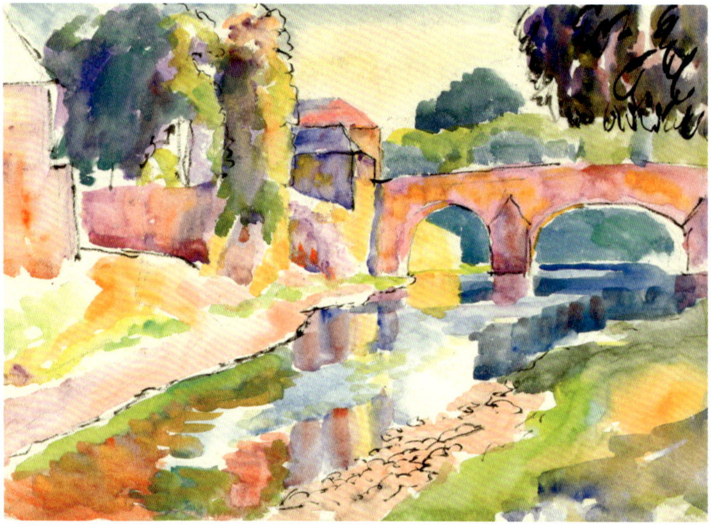

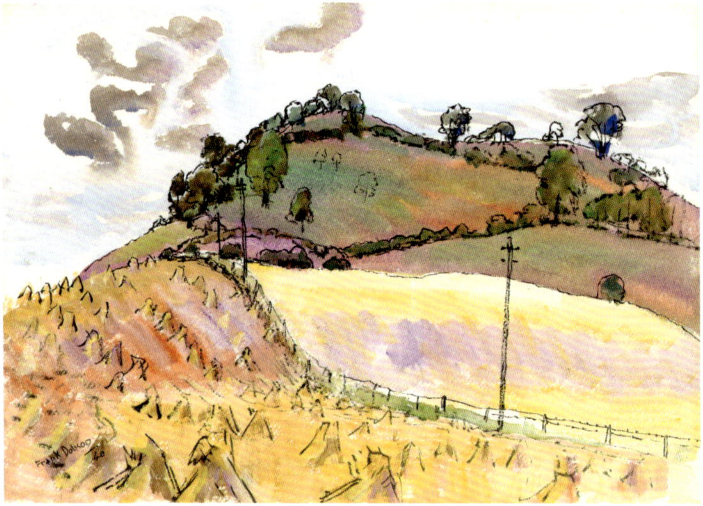

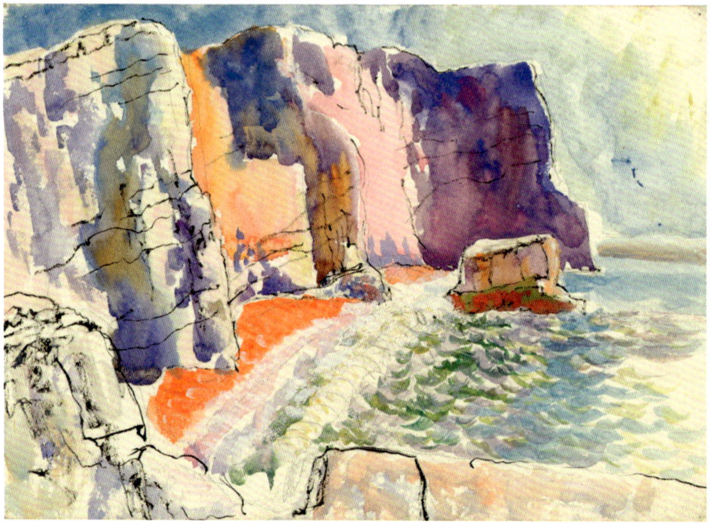

Landscape with Crane, watercolour, 25.5 x 35.5 cm
Bridge, watercolour, 25.5 x 35 cm
A Hillside in Wales, watercolour & ink, 1940, signed, 35.5 x 50 cm
Cliffs and Coastline, watercolour, 25.5 x 35.5 cm

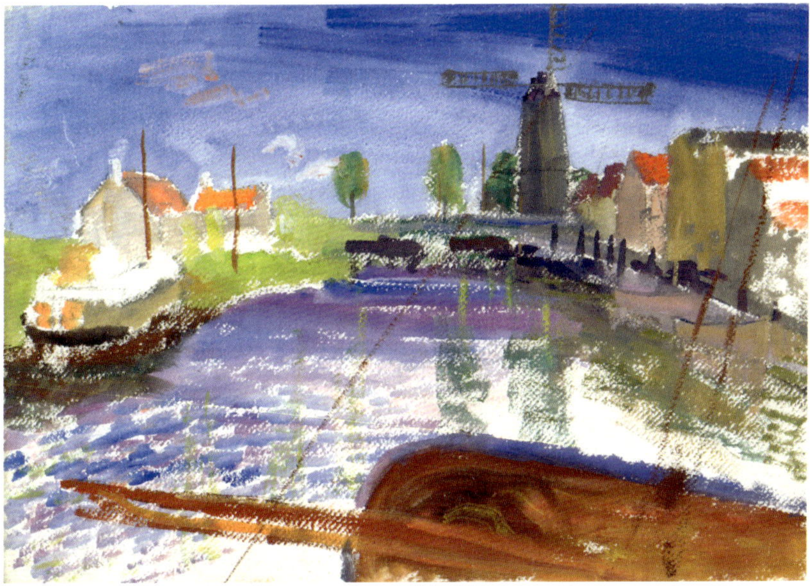

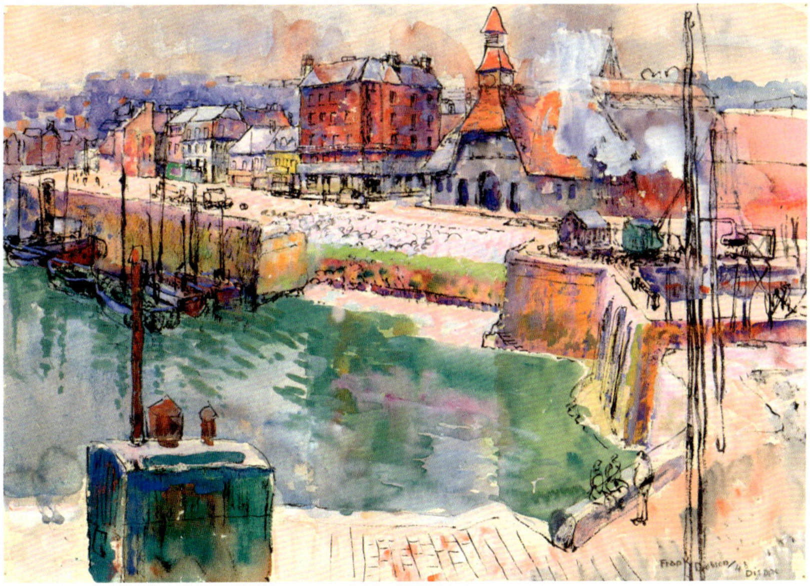

Windmill from the River, gouache, 35.5 x 50.5 cm
Dieppe Harbour, watercolour, 1948, signed, 33 x 45 cm

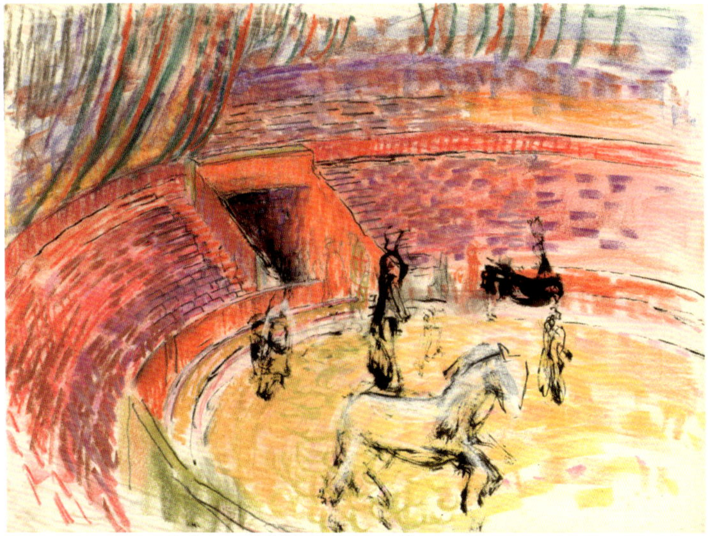

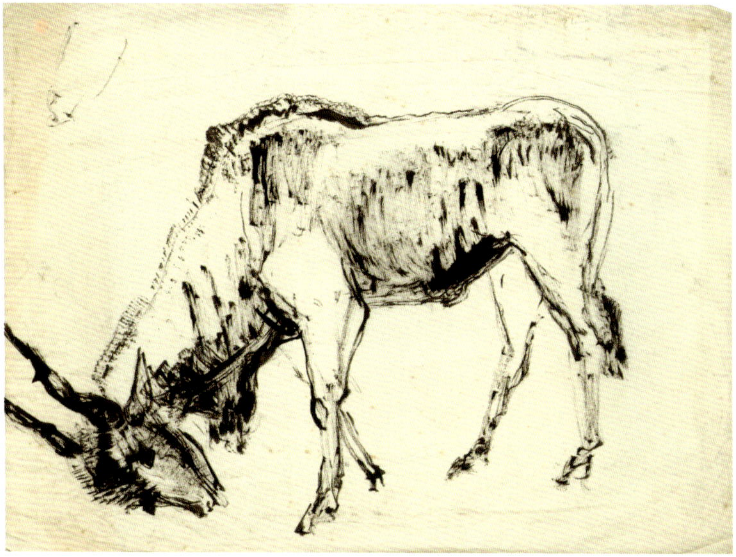

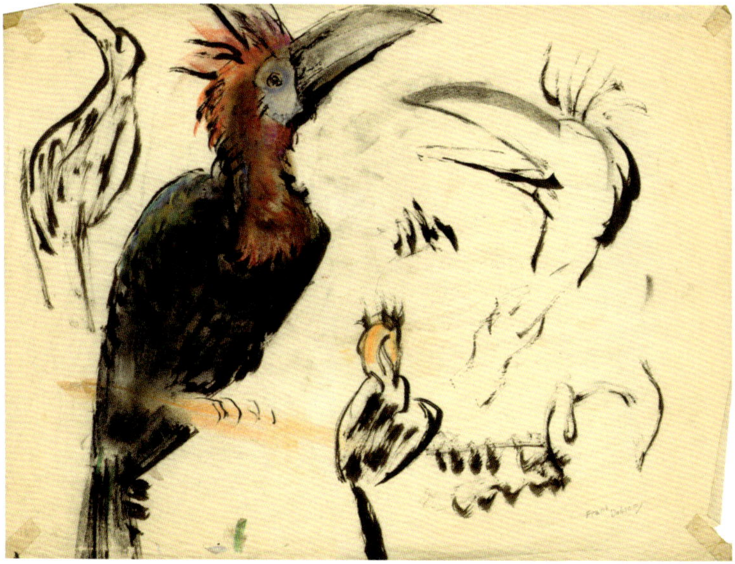

Circus Horses and Performers, chalk & ink, 37.5 x 50 cm
Bowing East African Eland Bull, ink, 31.5 x 43 cm
Wreathed Hornbill, chalk & ink, 37.5 x 50 cm

Exhibition Price List

*Prices are correct at October 2022 but will change due to increasing materials and casting costs

A Hillside in Wales	Watercolour & ink	£3,500
Arthur Houghton Jnr	Bronze	£15,000
At the Bar	Chalk	£2,500
At the Furnace	Chalk & charcoal	£2,250
Back of Seated Nude	Red chalk	£5,000
Bather with Towel	Chalk & charcoal	£4,000
Bowing East African Eland Bull	Ink	£1,500
Café Still Life	Chalk	£2,500
Café Still Life II	Chalk	£1,950
Circus Horses and Performers	Chalk & ink	£2,500
Cliffs and Coastline	Watercolour	£1,950
Crawling Woman	Bronze	£12,500
Crouching Nude	Bronze	£4,950
Dieppe Harbour	Watercolour	£3,500
Europa and the Bull	Bronze	£12,000
Freedom from Fear	Bronze	£17,500
Hand on Hip	Pen & ink	£5,500
Hop Pickers	Chalk	£950
Jigsaws	Chalk	£2,750
Kneeling Figure	Bronze	£12,500
Kneeling Torso	Bronze	£24,000
Lady Dorothea Ashley Cooper	Bronze	£35,000
Landscape with Crane	Watercolour	£1,950
Leaning Nude	Pencil	£4,000
Machinery	Chalk	£2,750
Morning	Bronze	£17,500
Mother and Child	Chalk & charcoal	£6,000
Naval Gunners	Gouache, watercolour & ink	£5,000
Noni	Bronze	£22,500
Noon	Bronze	£19,500
Nude Bending	Red chalk	£5,000
Nude from Behind	Charcoal	£6,000
Nude Torso	Chalk	£4,000
Peggy Salaman	Bronze	£19,500
Poplar Trees	Watercolour	£3,500
Portrait of Anne	Chalk	£3,500
Reclining Nude	Chalk	£6,000
Reclining Nude Figure	Bronze	£24,500
Recumbent Nude	Chalk & ink	£3,950
Recumbent Nude	Bronze	£5,500
Repast	Bronze	£17,500
Rhoda	Bronze	£27,000
Seated Figure	Red chalk	£5,000
Seated Leaning Figure	Bronze	£16,000
Seated Nude on a Chair	Bronze	£9,500
Sir Osbert Sitwell	Polished bronze	£85,000
Squatting Female Figure with Pitcher	Bronze	£24,500
Standing Nude	Red chalk & watercolour	£7,500
Standing Nude IV	Pencil	£4,000
Standing Torso (Study for Persephone 3)	Bronze	£16,000
Storm Wind	Watercolour & ink	£5,000
Study for Fount	Bronze	£14,000
Study for Large Group 2 (Two Friends)	Bronze	£9,500
Study for London Pride (Leisure 3)	Bronze	£19,500
Study for Persephone 1	Bronze	£1,750
Study for Standing Female Nude	Pen & ink	£7,500
Study for Toilet	Red chalk	£6,000
Study for Toilet 2	Bronze	£12,500
Study for Woman with a Bowl	Bronze	£14,000
Study of Standing Nude	Chalk & charcoal	£4,000
Terracotta Nude Facing Away	Red chalk	£6,000
The Belt	Chalk	£2,750
The Bridge	Watercolour	£1,950
The Nest	Bronze	£27,500
The Reader	Watercolour	£9,500
Tube Interiors III	Chalk	£1,500
Walking Nude	Chalk & pencil	£4,000
Windmill from the River	Gouache	£3,500
Woman Peeling an Apple (The Bastard)	Oil on canvas	£18,000
Woman Reclining	Red chalk	£5,000
Woman Seated	Bronze	£24,500
Woman with Fish II	Chalk & ink	£10,000
Woman with Scroll	Bronze	£12,500
Wreathed Hornbill	Chalk & ink	£1,950

Frank Dobson

Price List

October 2022

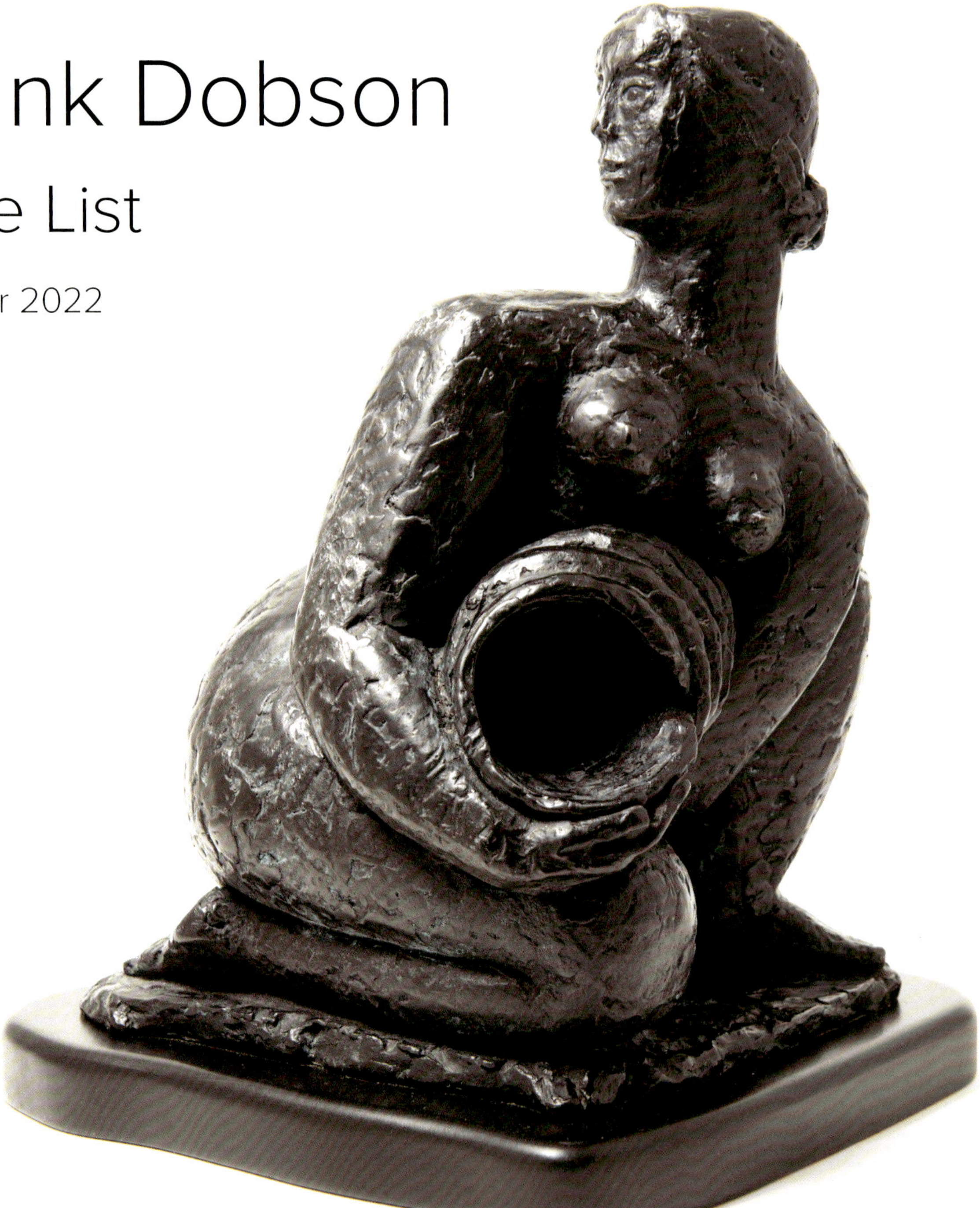

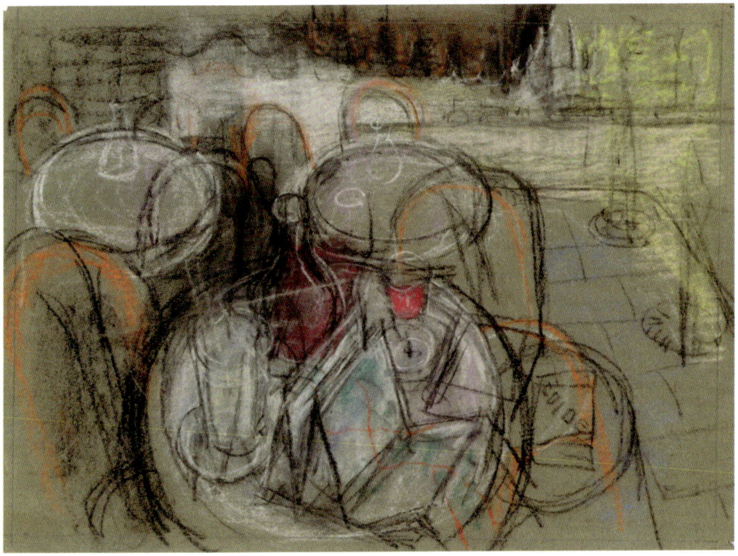

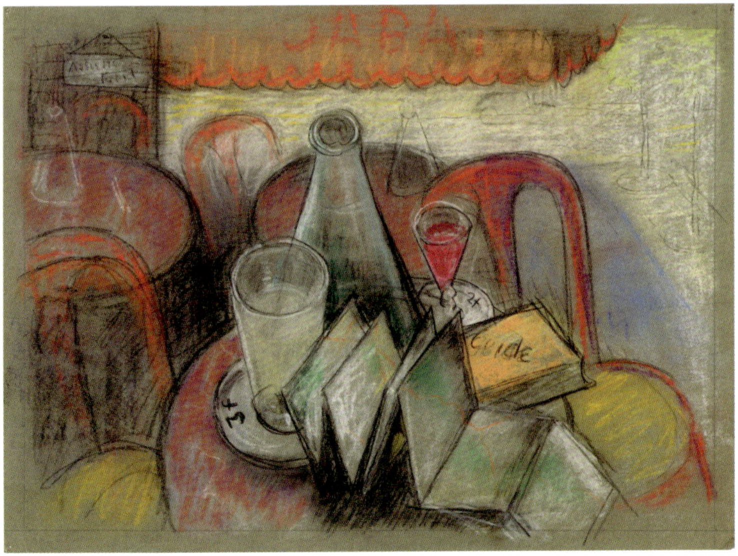

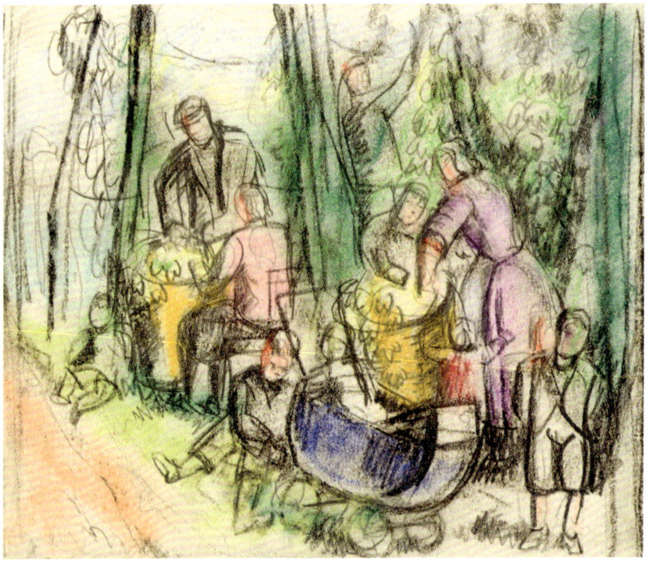

Café Still Life II, chalk, 25.5 x 35.5 cm
Café Still Life I, chalk, 25 x 35 cm
Hop Picking, chalk, estate stamp, 19 x 22.5 cm

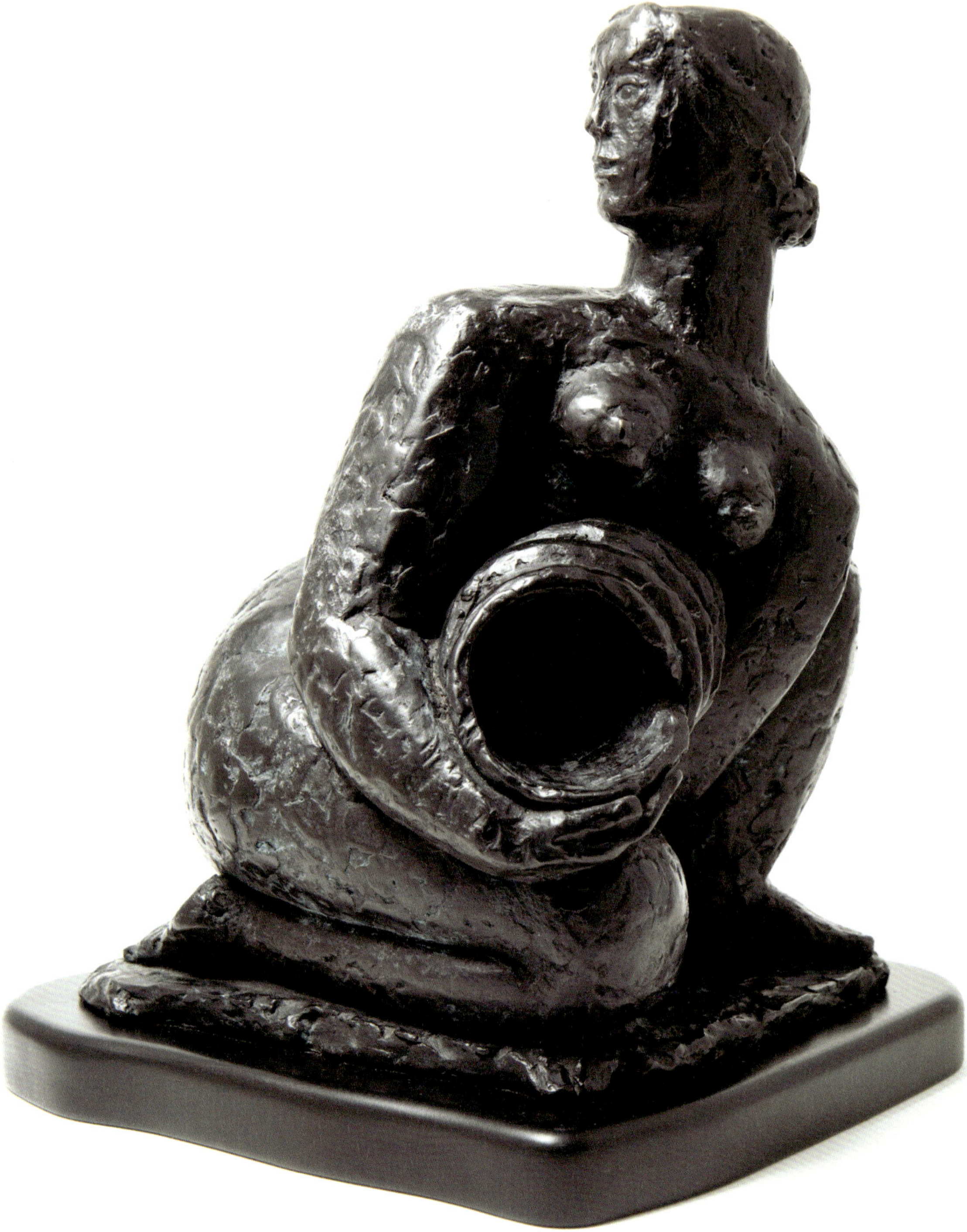

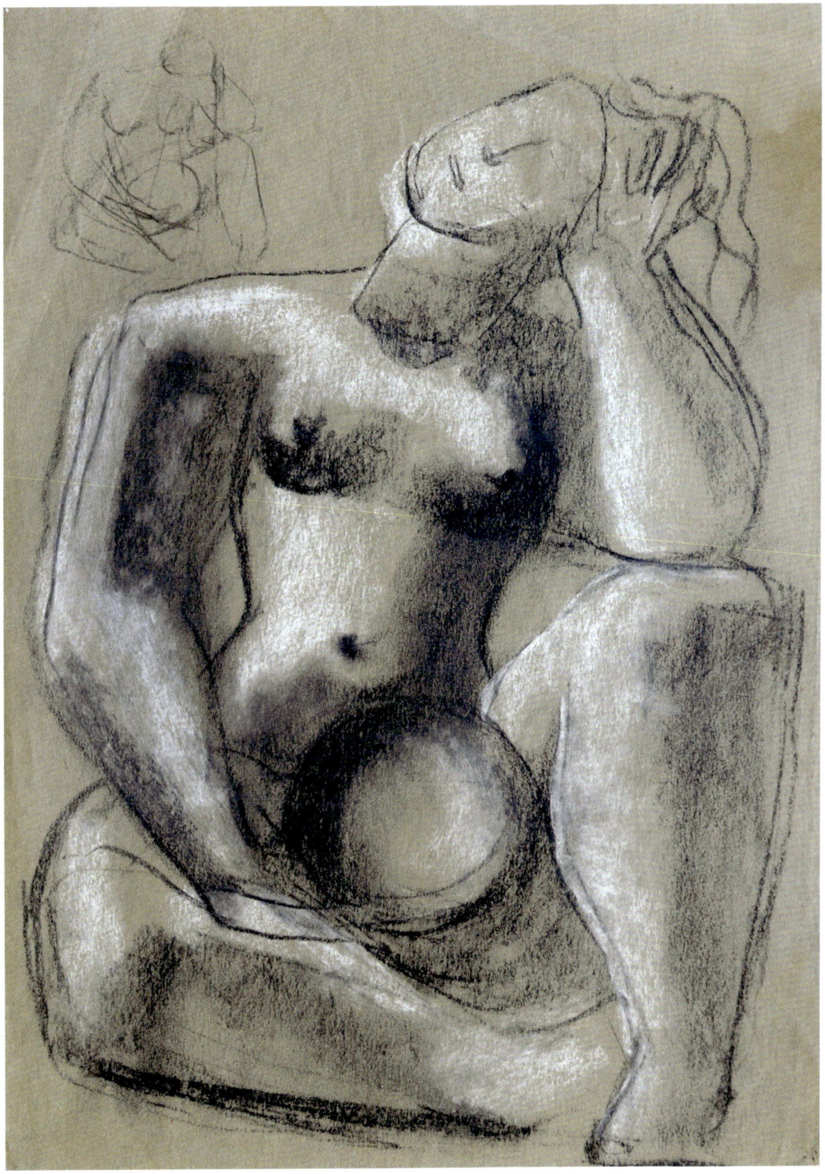

Squatting Female Figure with Pitcher, bronze, 2020, ed 12, estate stamp, h 39 cm
Cast from the unique estate bronze
Woman with Bowl, chalk, estate stamp verso, 38 x 28 cm

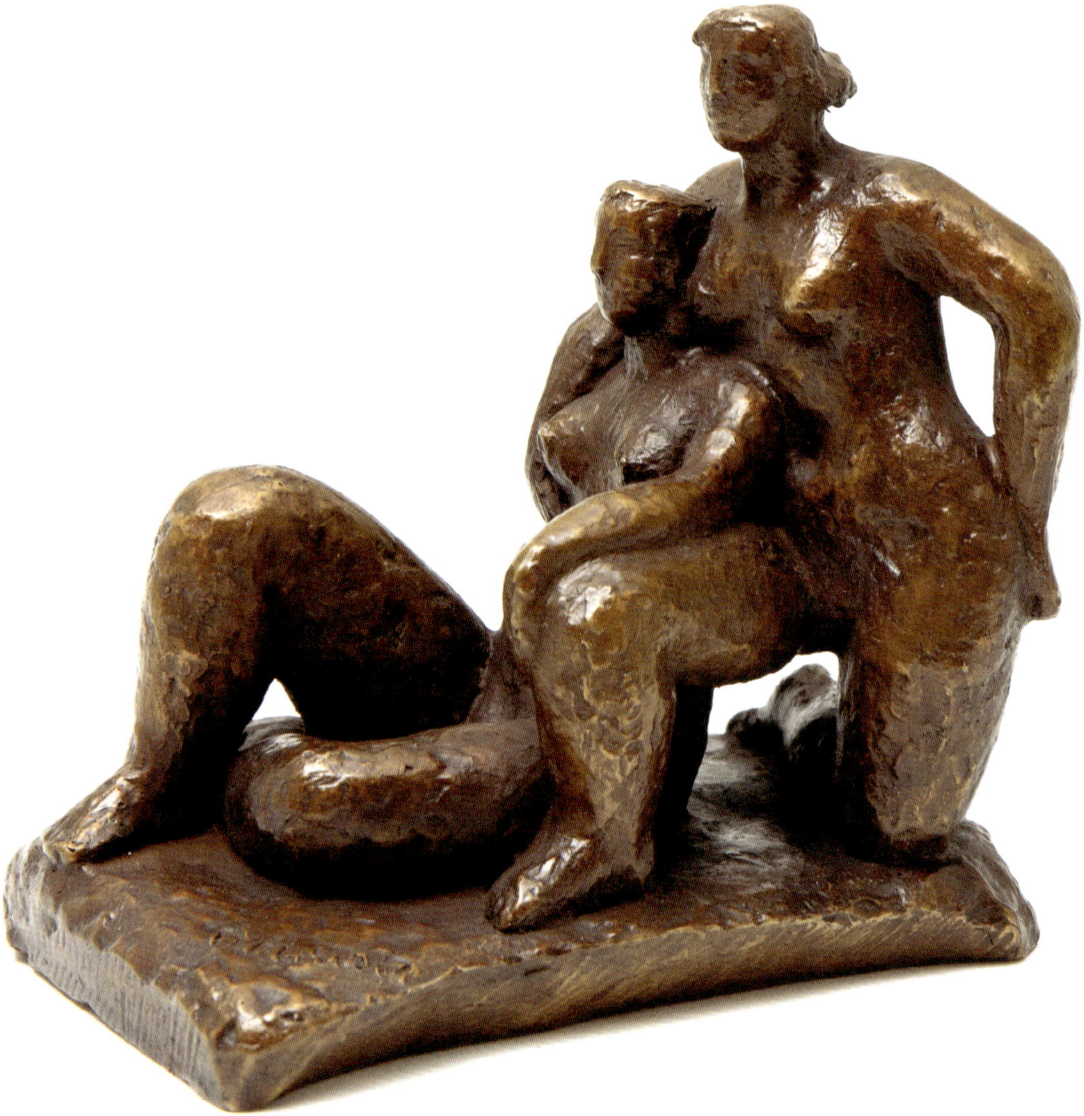

Meanwhile, he continued with his own work. *Study for Large Group 2 (Two Friends)*, a terracotta of 1940, now cast in a warm golden brown bronze, explores further the theme of two girls, reclining or sitting together, that we saw in *Noon*. In 1940 Dobson placed one figure behind the other, kneeling and supporting her friend. It's a strong and optimistic vision, admirably suited to wartime. A few years later, the subject has turned to single figures again: *Squatting Female Figure with Pitcher* (c1944), another unique terracotta now cast in bronze, and *Study for the Fount* (1944-5), which began as a unique hand-coloured plaster and is now cast in a resonant greeny-black bronze.

A later statement combines these two themes. *The Repast* (1946) features two women at right angles to each other with a large water jar between them. Again the original terracotta has now been cast in bronze, to great effect. The argument for casting Dobson's terracottas in bronze posthumously is a convincing one. It rests in the fact that this follows the natural progression, from study to finished sculpture, and that he would have cast the bronzes himself if he could have afforded it, but the high cost of materials all too often prevented him. This loss has now been made good by Goldmark and the artist's estate.

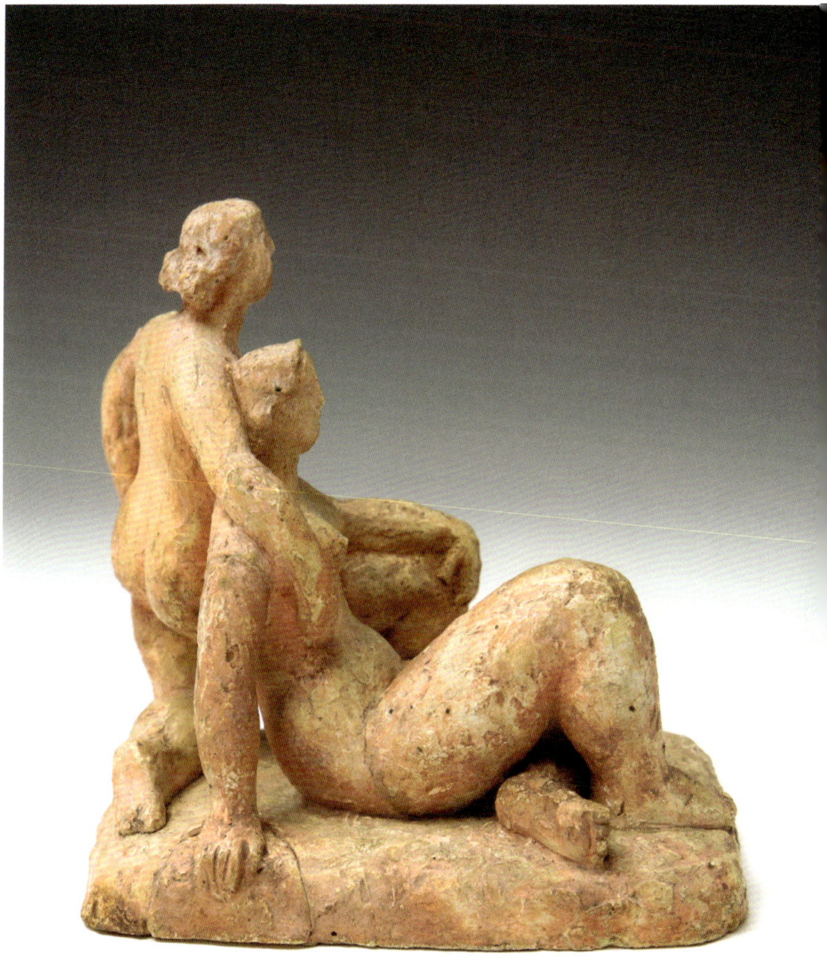

Study for Large Group 2 (Two Friends), bronze, 2018, ed 10, signed, h 14 cm
First casting from the 1944 terracotta
Study for Large Group 1, polychrome plaster, 1940, h 14 cm

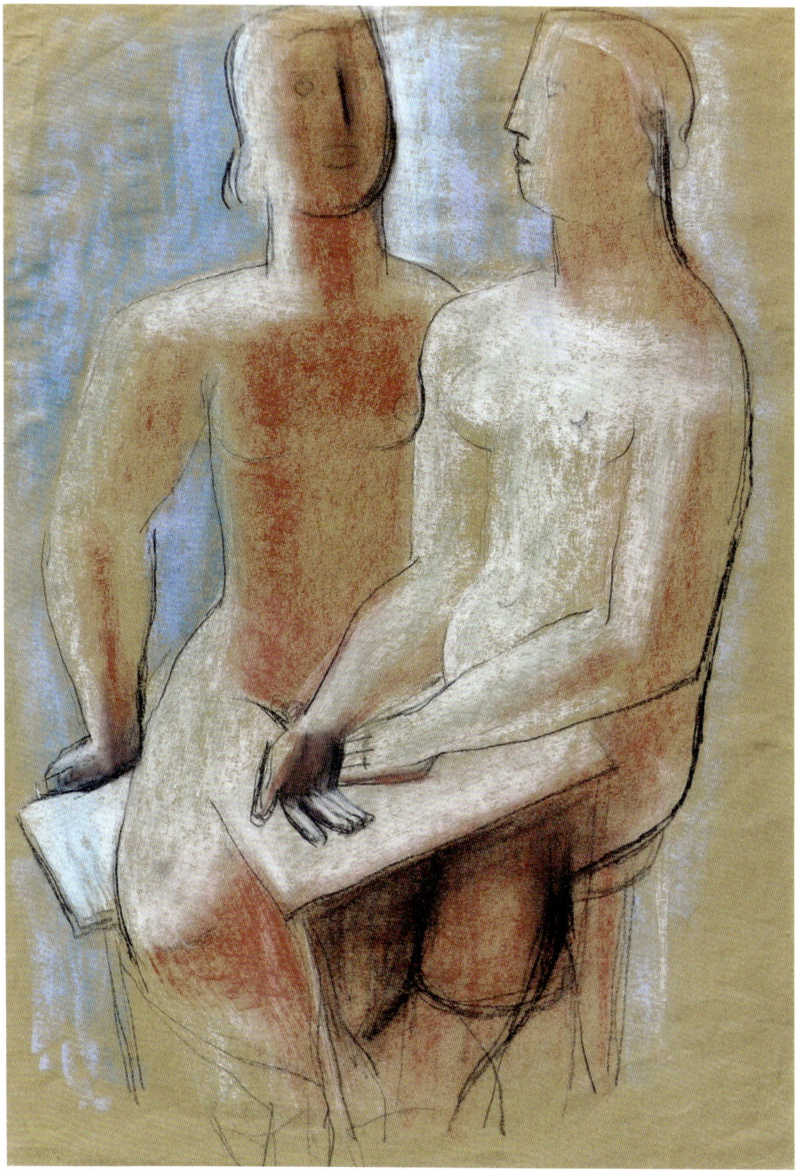

Study for Sculpture (Two Figures), chalk, 56 x 38 cm
The Repast, bronze, 2020, ed 12, estate stamp, h 36 cm
Cast from the 1946 terracotta

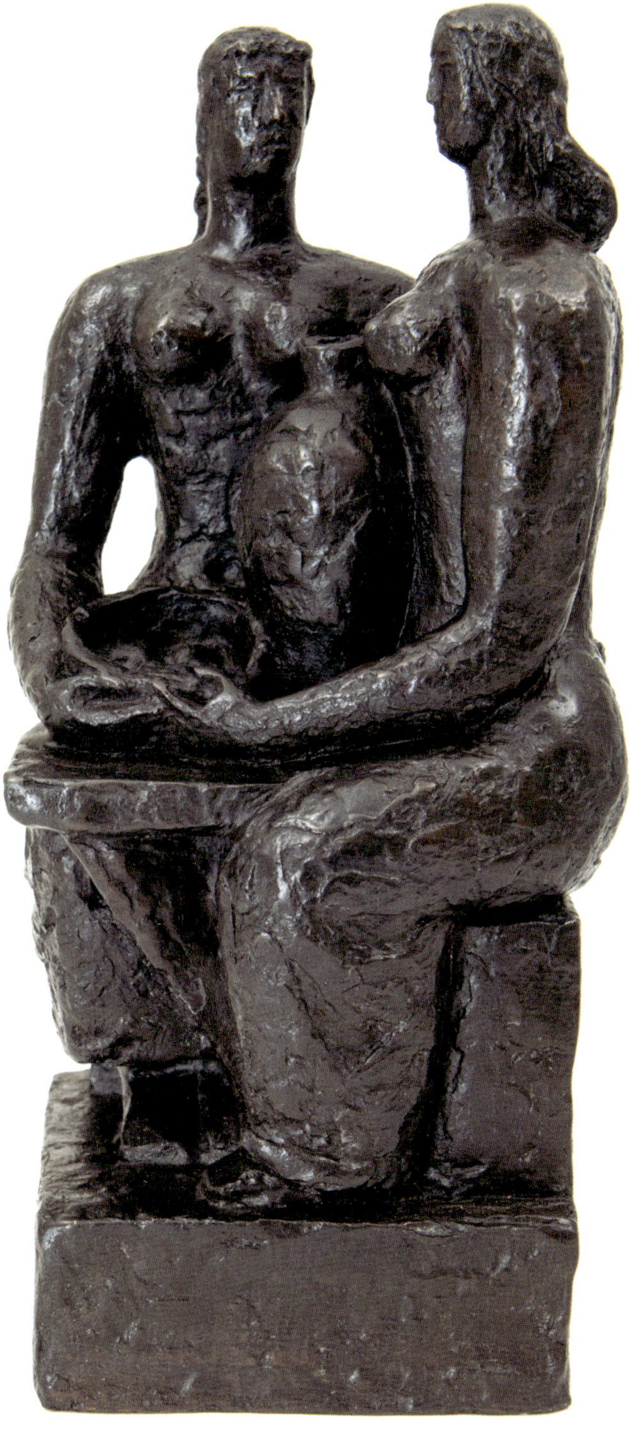

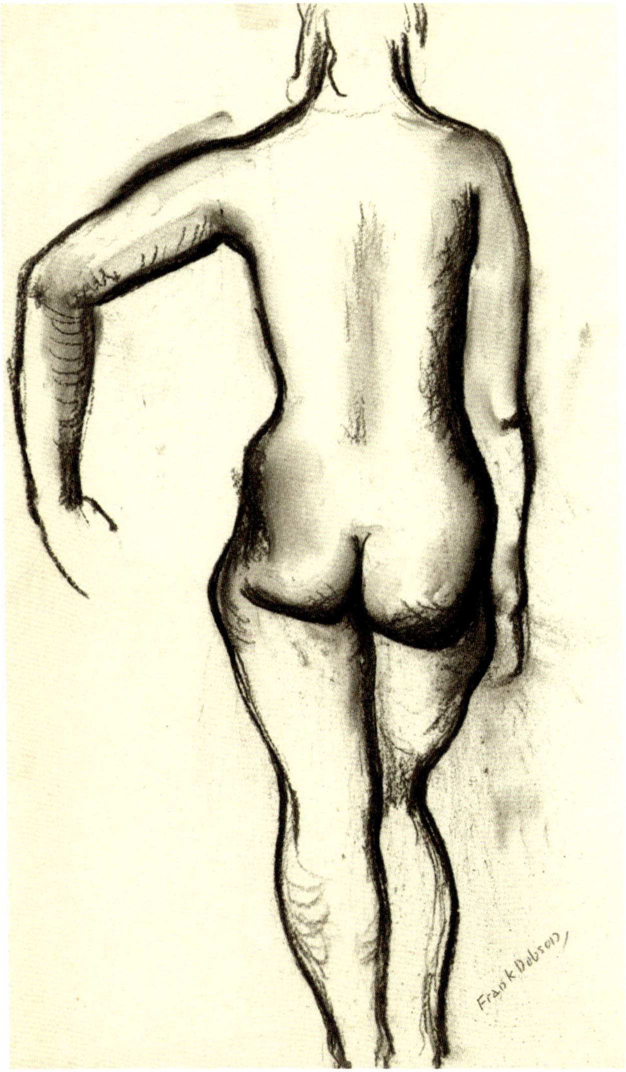

During these years, Dobson had moved out of London, first to Bristol (where he was given a major retrospective exhibition at the Museum and Art Gallery), and then to Hampshire. Understandably, his first priority was for the safety of his wife and daughter, and the move proved prescient: tragically, his Manresa Road studio was bombed and burnt out during the Blitz, and a huge amount of work was lost. Oddly, he never went back or tried to salvage anything from the ruins, though according to his students there was work which could have been saved or re-built. Perhaps he was already feeling ill at ease in the modern world, and could not view the future with his habitual optimism.

In many ways, his work was now against the temper of the times. His life-affirming Mediterranean paganism did not accord well with ration books and khaki, or indeed with Francis Bacon's epochal *Three Studies for Figures at the Base of a Crucifixion* which had just been painted. In a wartime talk Dobson called for Peace Monuments to be built, rather along the lines of wayside shrines, as a more encouraging alternative to War Memorials. An engaging idea, but not one seized upon by the commissioning authorities.

'Walking in the Fulham Road ... met Frank

Nude from Behind, charcoal, signed, 51 x 29 cm
Study for *Fount*, bronze, 2018, ed 10, estate stamp, h 23 cm
Cast from the 1944/5 plaster

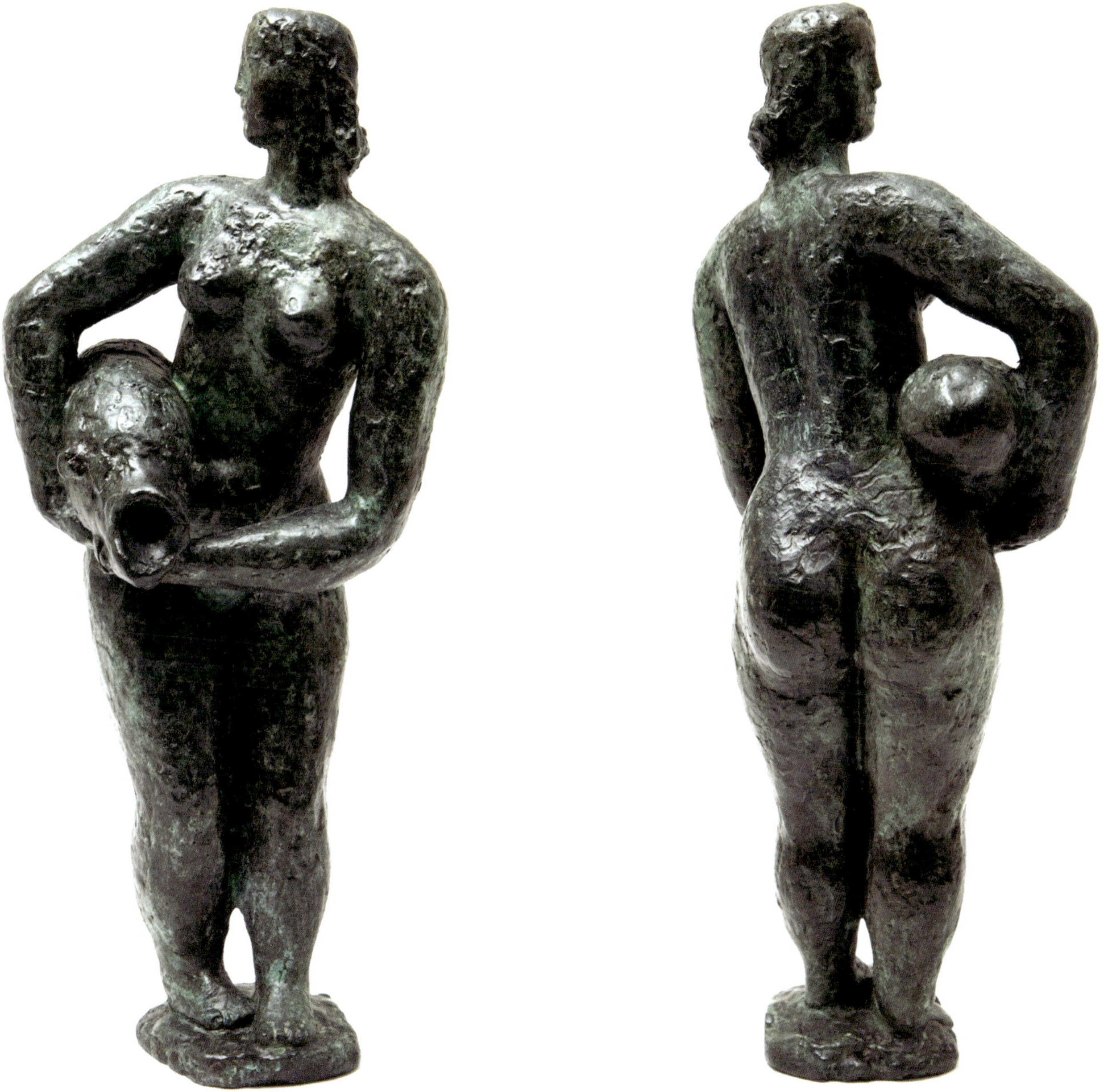

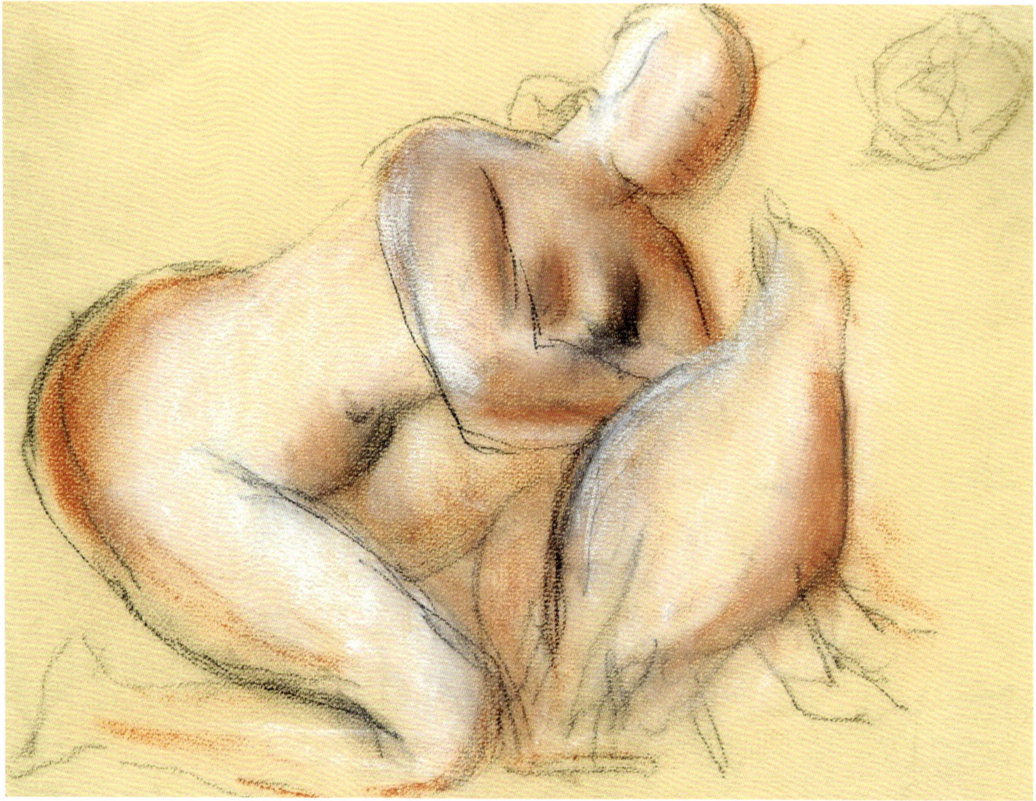

Dobson, who is staying in one of the Avenue Studios which belongs to a pupil of his. He is made uncomfortable by the pessimism of Picasso, and hates post-War conditions — starting life again... He is teaching drawing one day a week at the Central School...' Randolph Schwabe confided to his journal in December 1945. Dobson had another decade of work in him, much of which was to be spent happily teaching at the Royal College of Art (he was a popular professor there), but already he was feeling old, and as if his moment had passed.

Crouching Nude with Bird, chalk, estate stamp, 23.8 x 31 cm
Freedom from Fear, bronze, 2021, ed 12, estate stamp, h 23 cm
Cast from the 1941 terracotta

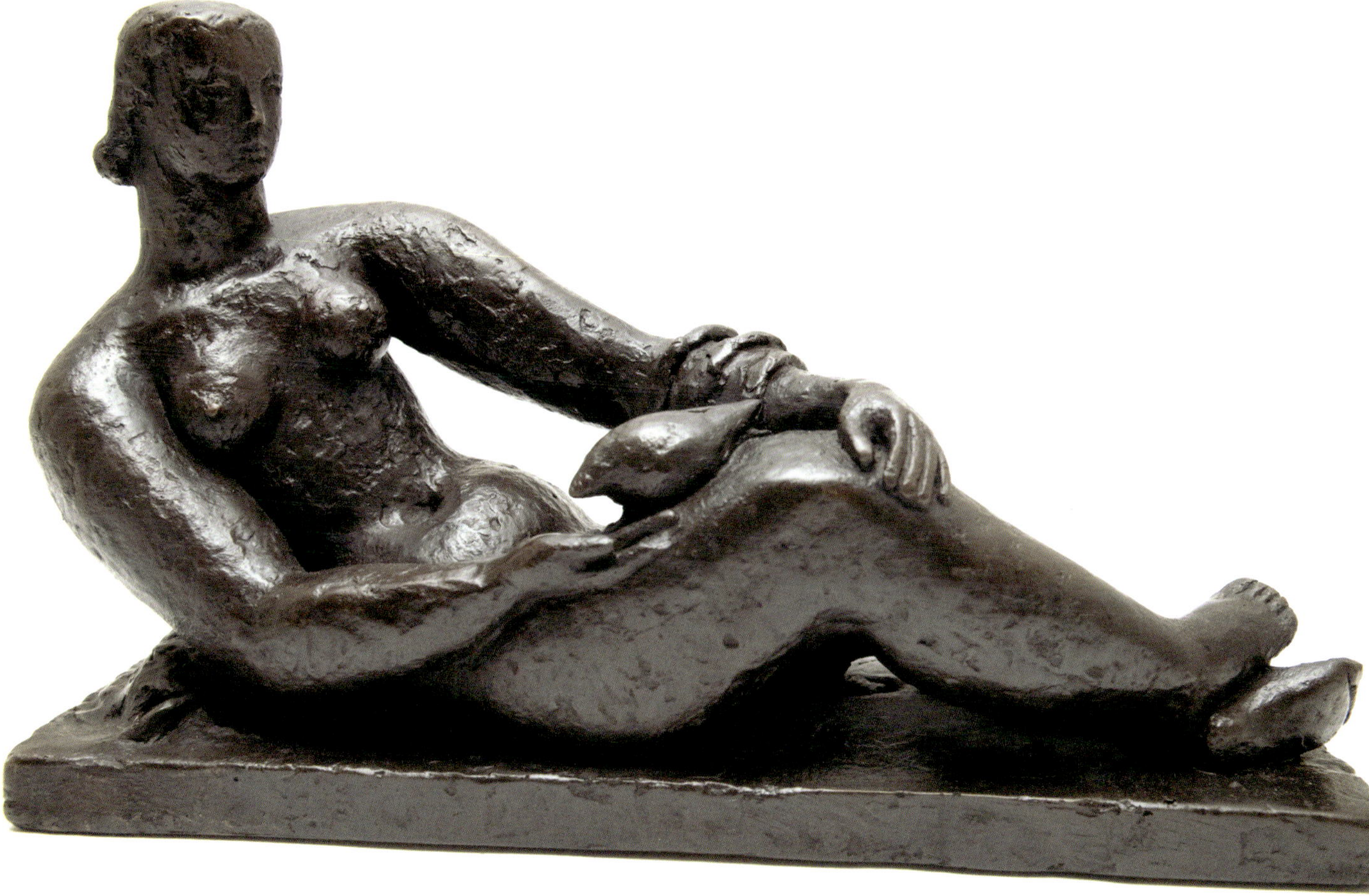

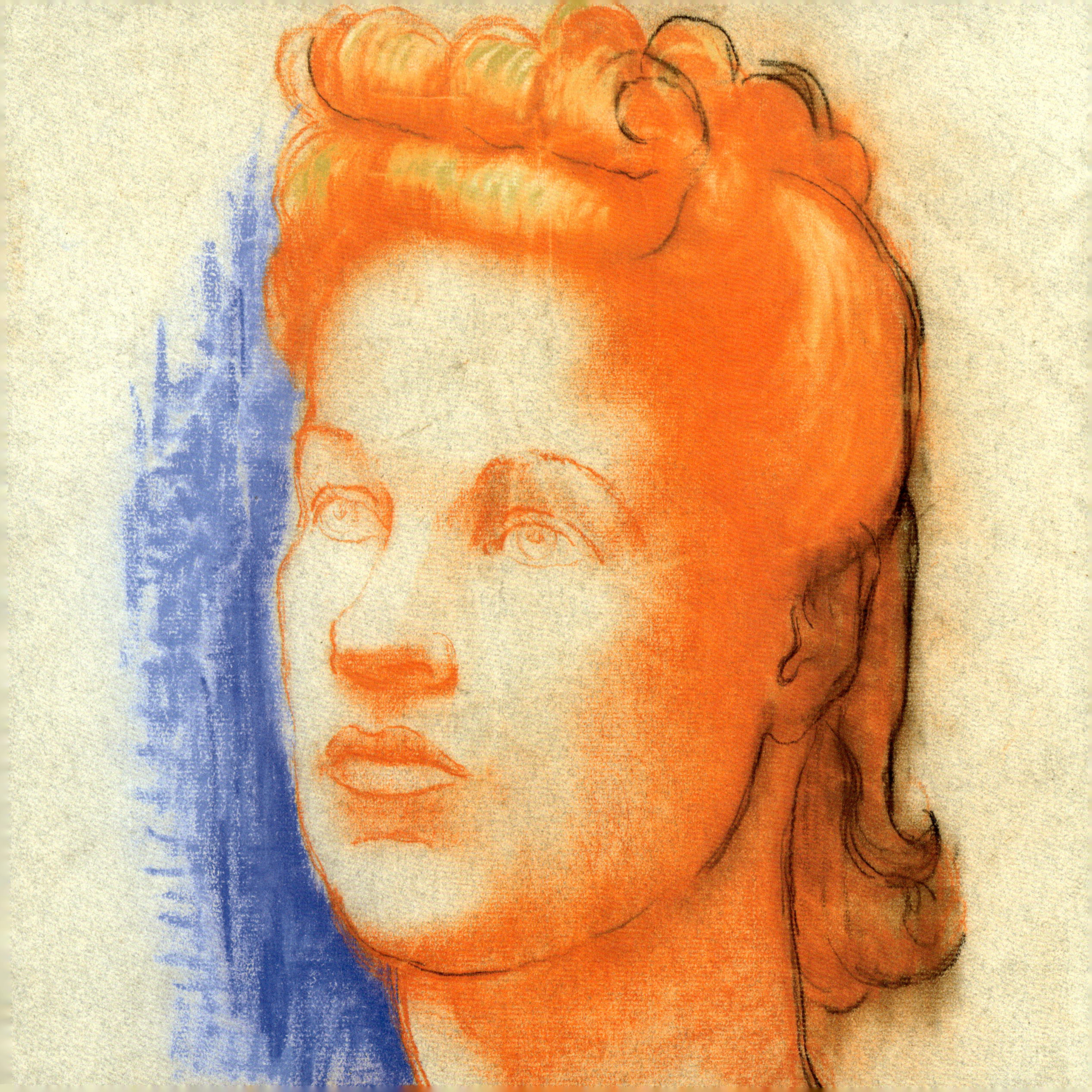

5

Drawing & Later Work (1946-63)

Portrait of Anne, chalk, c.1940s, estate stamp verso, 48 × 31 cm

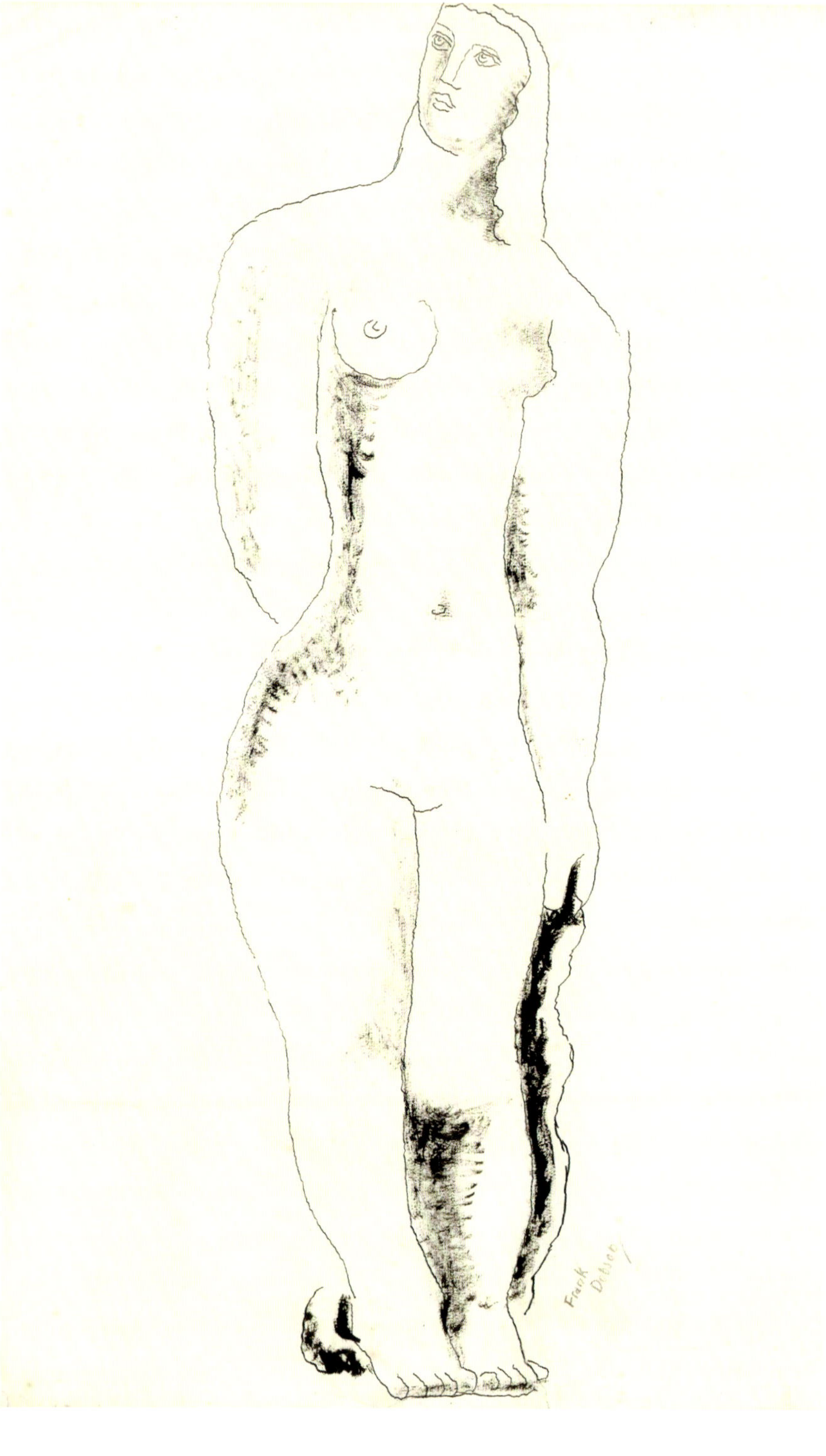

'The psychological element should not be lost sight of, but it should be subordinated to the aesthetic.'

Frank Dobson

Dobson was a prolific and accomplished draughtsman, and because his drawing was at the heart of his creative process, it is only fitting to devote a separate section to it here. Collectors may own a distinctive Dobson red chalk drawing of a girl, and thus possess a typical work by a master of 20th century British art.

The drawings of Watteau, Fragonard and Alfred Stevens were influential exemplars for the style of sanguine, or red chalk, drawing that became Dobson's trademark. Although he also drew in ink and graphite, Dobson used red chalk predominantly, with the occasional touch of black or some other colour. (He did not whole-heartedly adopt the French method of 'three chalks' — red, black and white — pioneered by Rubens but made famous by the drawings of Fragonard and Boucher.) Besides various weights and shades of white paper he would sometimes use grey-green, tan or pale olive sheets, on which he would perhaps draw in black outlines with the volume modelled in white. In some of the drawings (particularly the ink ones) there are edging bands of another colour to throw the flesh of the model into relief. (He would use purple, yellow, red and black for this.) The purpose was twofold, to introduce an eye-catching decorative element into the composition as well as to provide a spatial context.

Dobson drew principally to gather information for his sculptures, and it is worth observing here how directly his red chalk drawings translate into the red clay of his terracotta maquettes. Thus, for the most part, his drawings are working drawings. One or two of the more finished nudes were made as presentation drawings for exhibition and sale, for example *Drawing for Romantic* (1935), and *Persephone* (1930s), both striking images. There is a primitive confrontational quality to these figures which moves away from representational drawing towards a style driven by ideas more than observation. This aspect of Dobson's work existed in parallel to his more naturalistic

Study for Standing Female Nude, pen & ink, 1930s, signed, 62 x 22 cm

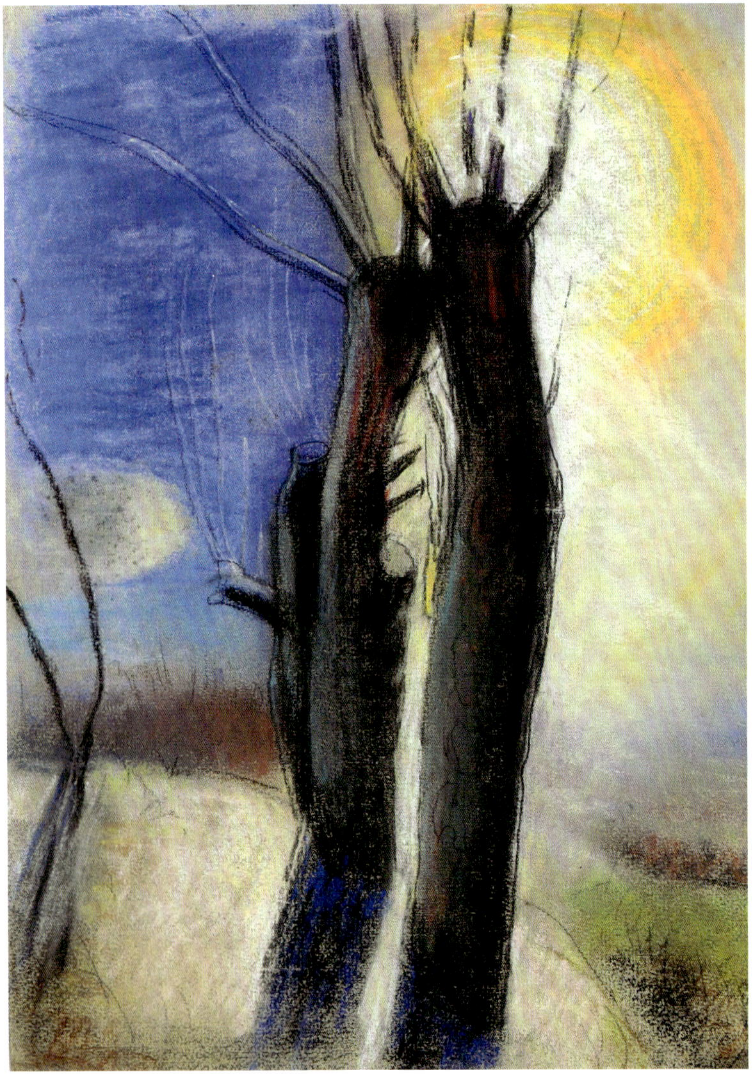

approach, but each could enrich and enhance the other.

Dobson liked to draw and paint trees: there are red chalk sculptural drawings of tree trunks as well as brightly coloured gouaches. He drew groups of trees from a distance, or sections of bole and branch in close-up, lavished with colour, sometimes bringing the sky down in great reflected puddles around their roots. He would mould the foliage into unexpectedly solid-looking shapes, great sculptural masses of colour. The wartime landscape gouaches are full of summer light and optimism, showing traces of the exotic colour of Gauguin, much-loved by Dobson since he first encountered it. Half-a-dozen poplars in a colourful landscape (greens, blues, pinks, reds) contrast with a trio of pollarded willows by a river. Blue and purple shadows abound.

However, Dobson is not celebrated for his landscapes, but for his figure work. (It should be noted, however, that if he sometimes drew and sculpted the legs and torsos of his women like tree trunks, he also returned the compliment: his trees often resemble the human form.) His confident use of outline derives from Ingres, and even its occasional mutation into a sensitive hesitancy has the immediacy of direct observation. In graphite drawings he could make

Dark Trees and Sunlight, chalk, 31.7 x 24 cm
Large Trees (detail), watercolour, gouache & ink, 57 x 80 cm

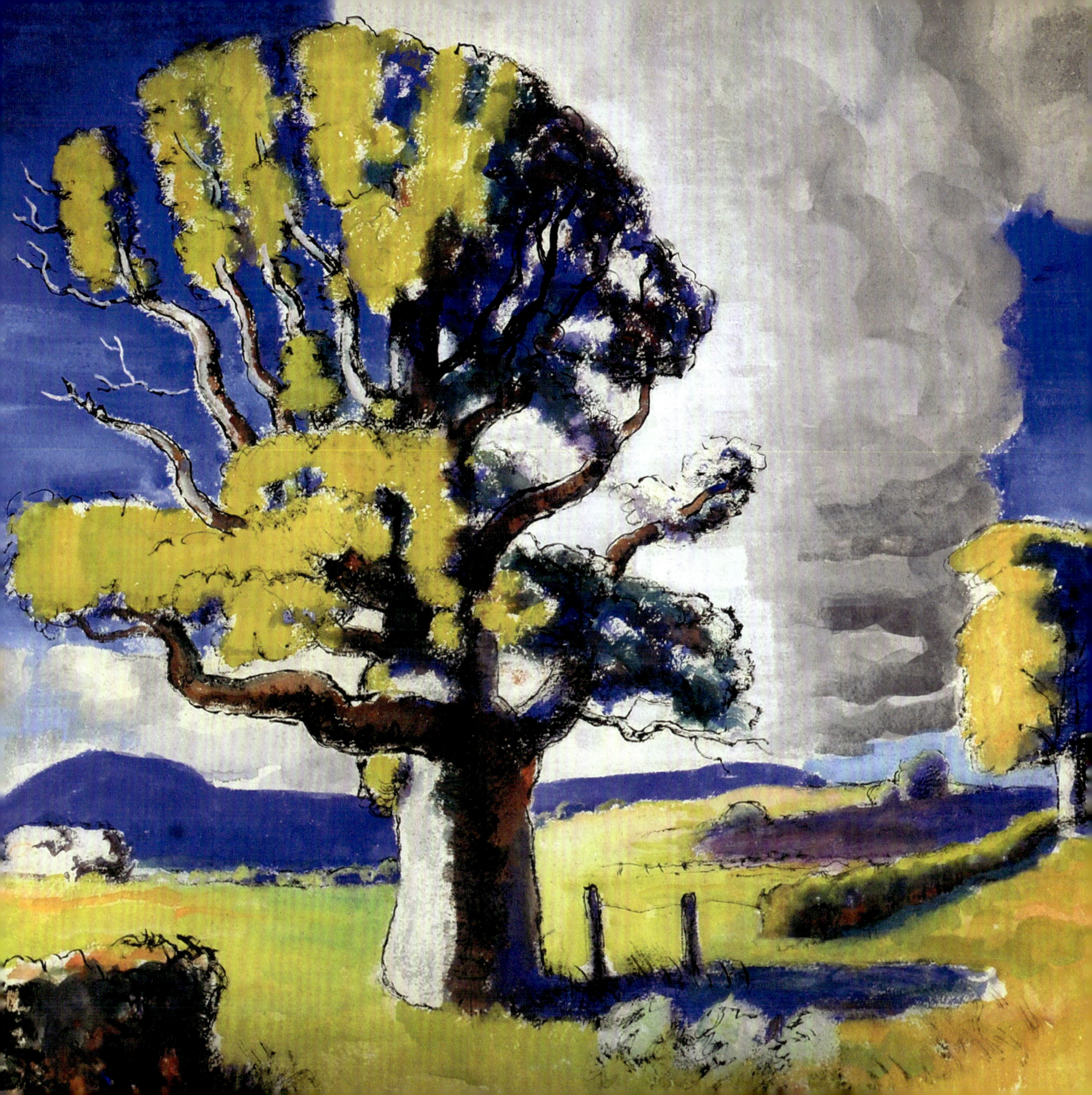

Frank Dobson

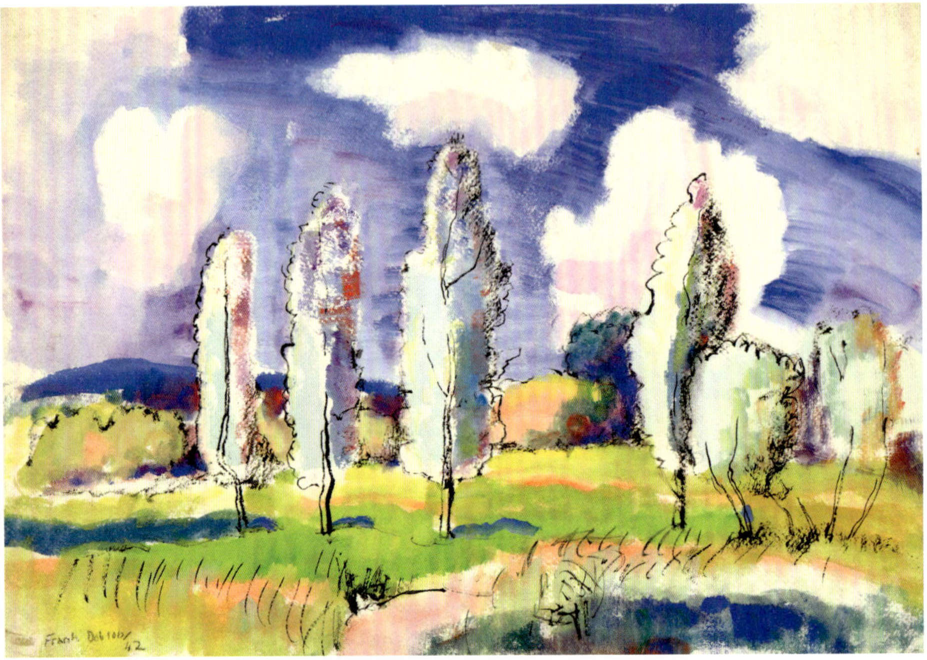

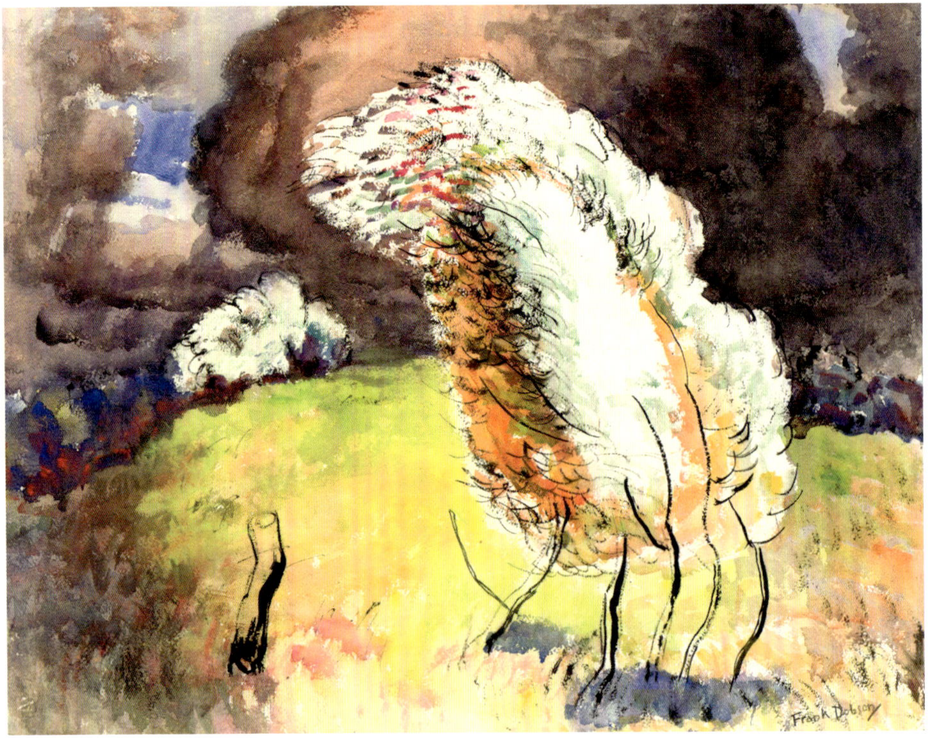

Poplar Trees,
watercolour & ink, 1942, signed, 35.5 x 51 cm
Storm Wind,
watercolour & ink, signed, 44 x 55.5 cm

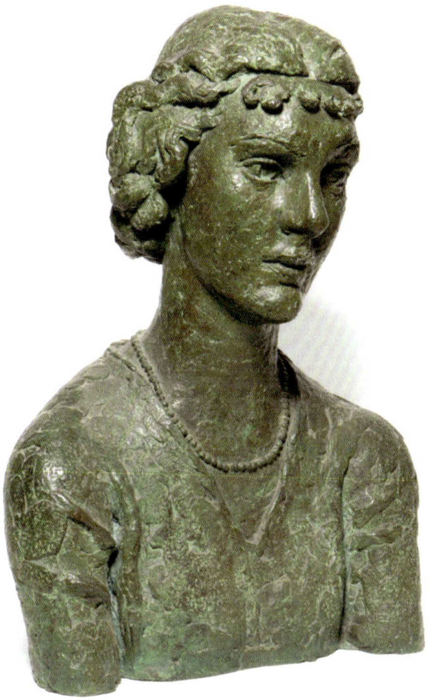

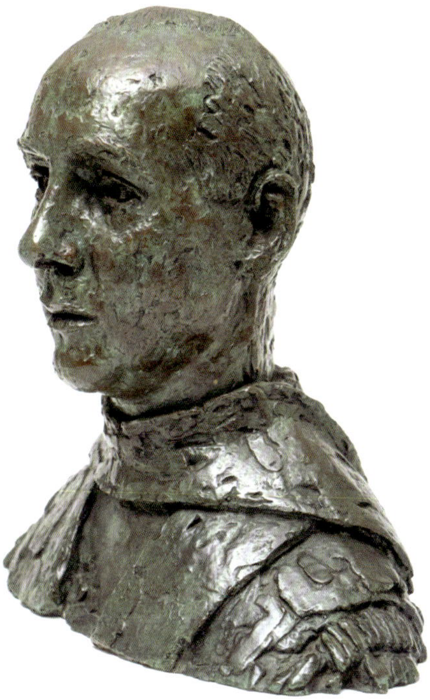

effective use of smudging to evoke volume, a practice that doubtless derived from his training in stump drawing at Hospitalfield.

The graphite portrait of Tommy Earp (presumably dating from the 1920s, judging by the youthfulness of the sitter), Dobson's brother-in-law, is a fine sensitive piece of outline drawing. Fluid and economic in character, neither sentimentalised nor idealised, it is a good foil to Augustus John's more romantic painted studies of their mutual friend. Another drawing, this time in red chalk, of Dennis Browne, Marquis of Sligo, done in 1937 is very strong, as is *Portrait of Anne* (Dobson's daughter) from the 1940s, in sanguine, black chalk and pencil. These are carefully individualised renditions, not studies of a physical type that appealed to him, but truthful accounts of character and personality.

Peggy Salaman, unique bronze, 1934, h 61 cm
Commissioned by the sitter, Peggy Salaman was the aviatrix who beat the London to Cape Town light aeroplane record, 1931

Arthur Houghton Jr, unique bronze, 1953, signed, h 46 cm
This magnificent bust of the celebrated businessman and philanthropist who endowed the Houghton Library at Harvard was modelled during Dobson's brief visit to the States in 1953

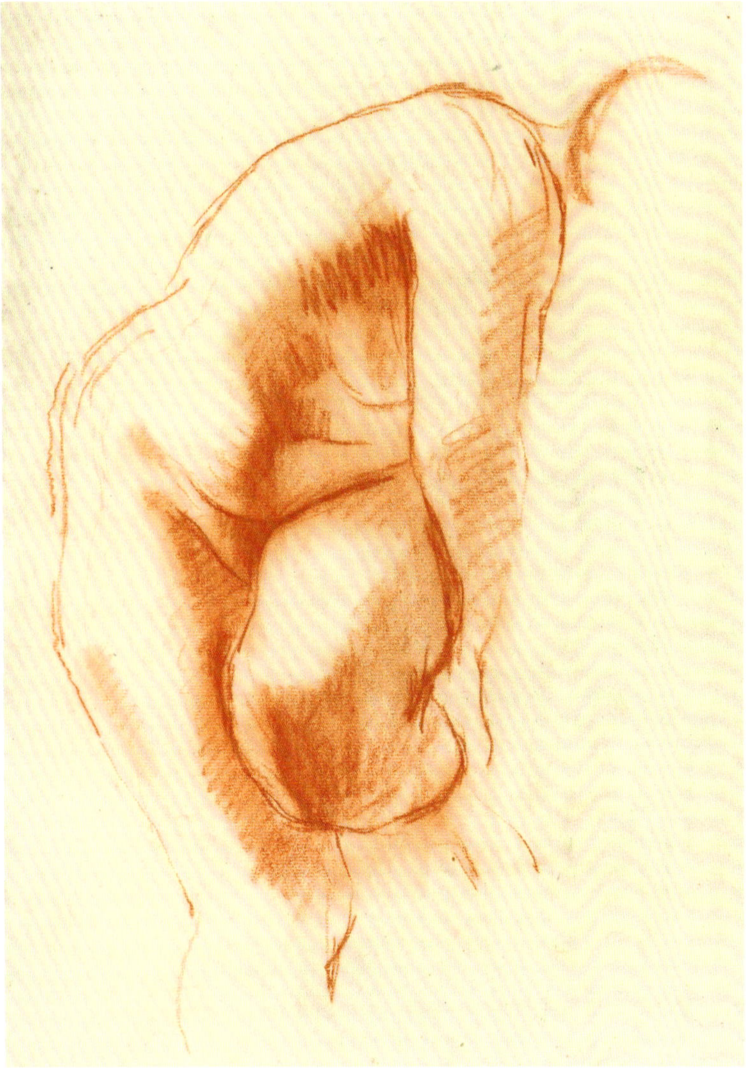

Portraiture represented a substantial part of his output and was a useful source of income, but the quintessential Dobson subject remains the female nude. There is a beautiful and very effective red chalk study of a girl with one massive knee up. The consequent changes in tension across her stomach, pelvis and torso are exquisitely yet simply captured. A smallish nude drawing shows a model with black hair standing out stiff from her head in corkscrews, like electrified dreadlocks. This is a real mixed media composition, employing pencil, ink and blue, turquoise, pink, red, purple, white and black chalk, and offering an unusually detailed face for a change. (Dobson usually concentrated his formidable powers on the depiction of the body, giving little attention to the facial features.) Another maverick piece is a magnificent 1947 study of a pair of knees held demurely together, allowing Dobson to focus on the ensuing shapes made by legs and feet.

Standing Nude (1935) is in red chalk but has an edge of brushy gouache colour, purple and grey, down her left side to accentuate the form. Another drawing from 1935 is entitled *Drawing for Romantic*, two girls in a close and friendly embrace, side by side, holding hands, with an aura of pink gouache surrounding them. Red ink

Nude Bending, red chalk, estate stamp verso, 39 x 26.5 cm
Standing Nude, red chalk & watercolour, 50 x 35 cm

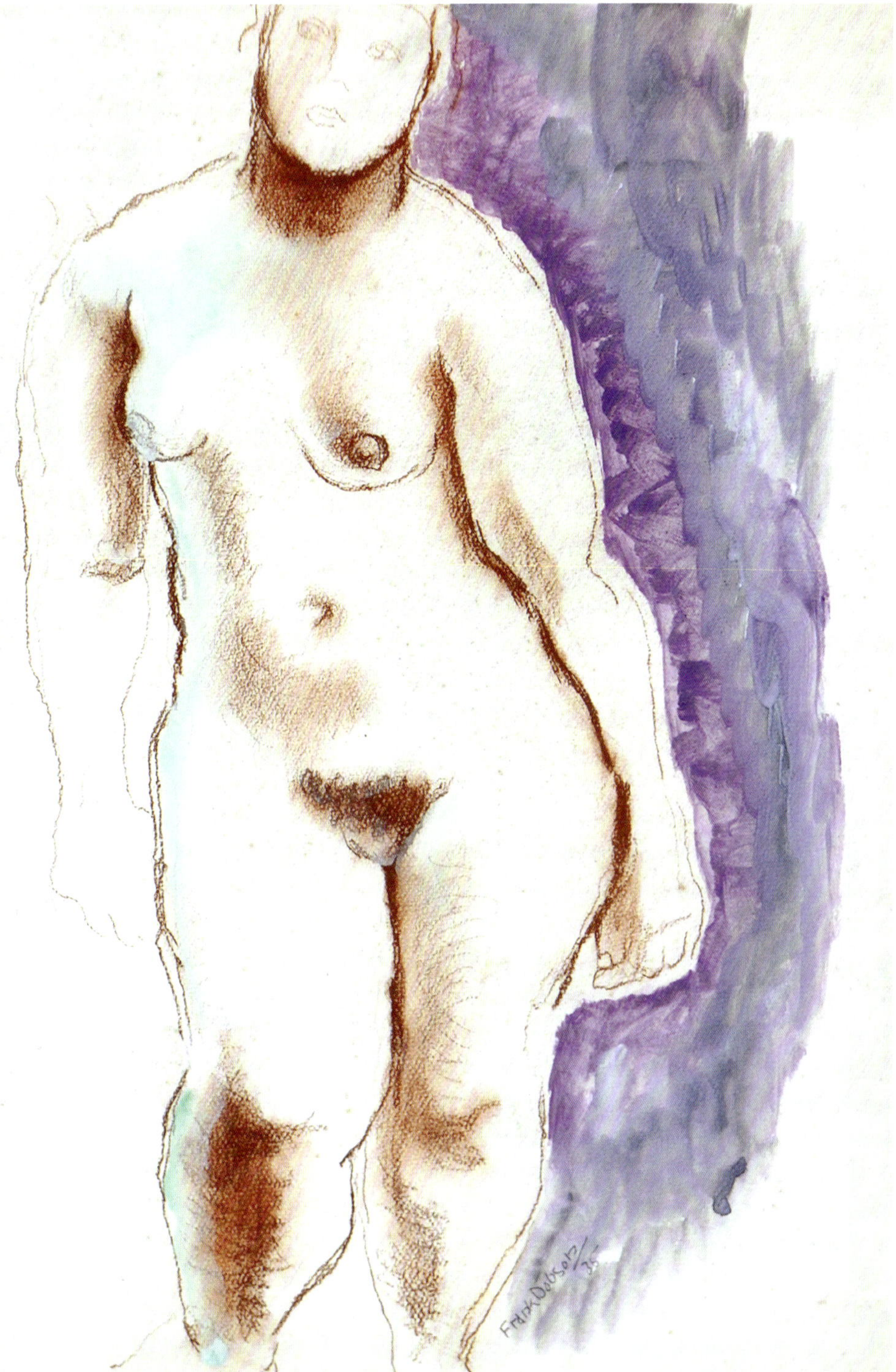
Frank Dobson/35

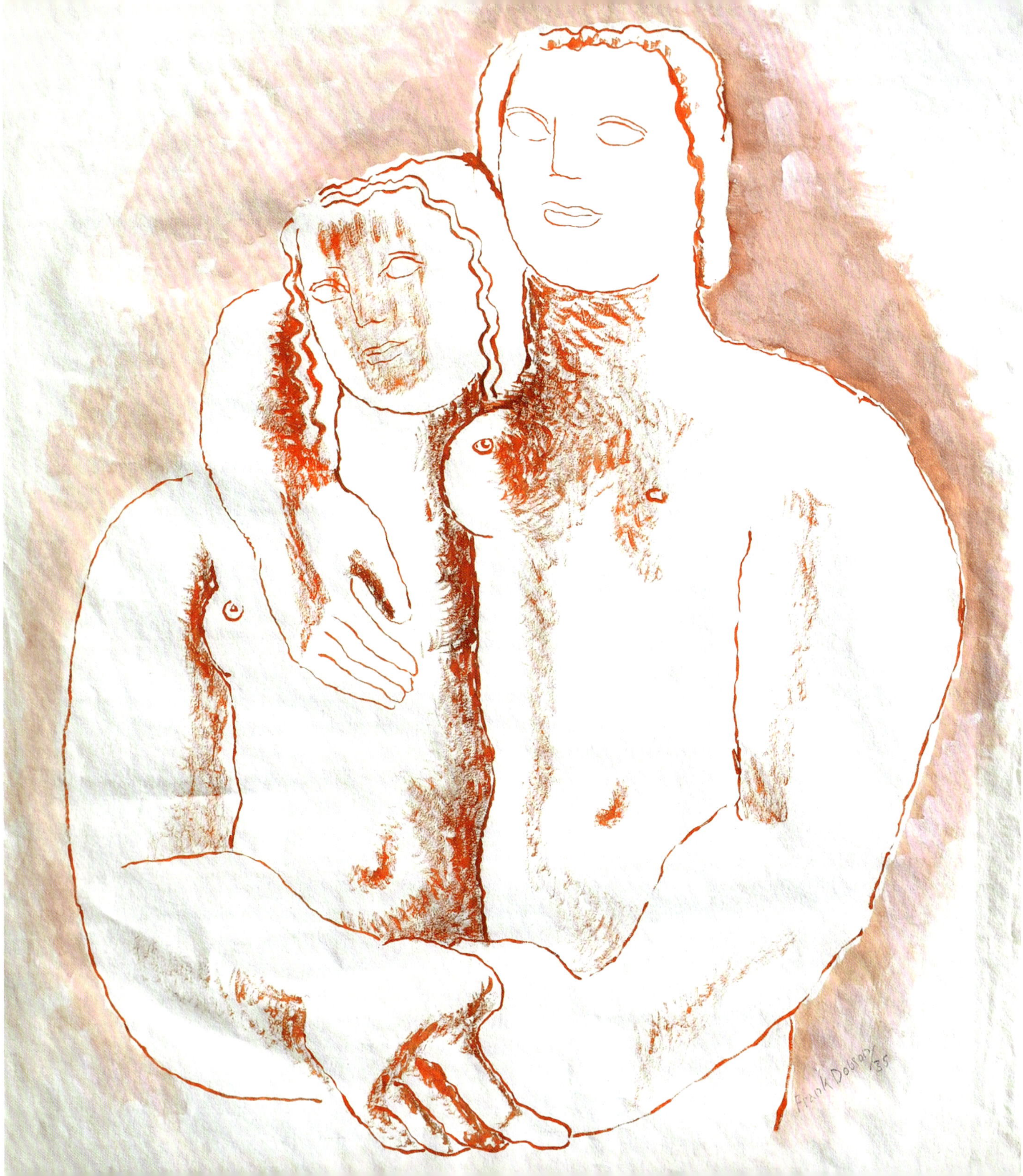
Frank Dobson/35

or paint is employed for the outlines, and possibly some chalk for the volumetric marks. This image has an archaic, primitive quality, which shifts it away from direct observation towards the abstraction of an idea. (*Romantic* is the title of a lost 1935 Ancaster stone sculpture. There is another sculpture on this theme, a small bronze from the same year, known as *Study for Romantic*.)

A drawing of a long thin, attenuated torso, probably dating from the 1930s, harks back to Dobson's 1921 sculpture *Giraffe Torso*, and to another Portland stone torso from 1928; also to the *Manresa Venus (Charnaux Venus)* of 1933 now in the Tate. In its expressive red-orange, purple and black chalks, with touches of white, it is also related to the study for *Persephone*, another 1930s drawing, a black ink, half-draped figure with brushy blue gouache behind her. In the attenuated torso drawing there is a secondary figure to the right, an echo of the main figure with the same jutting breasts, carried out crisply in terse strokes of black chalk. This is oddly reminiscent of the much later work of Kenneth Armitage.

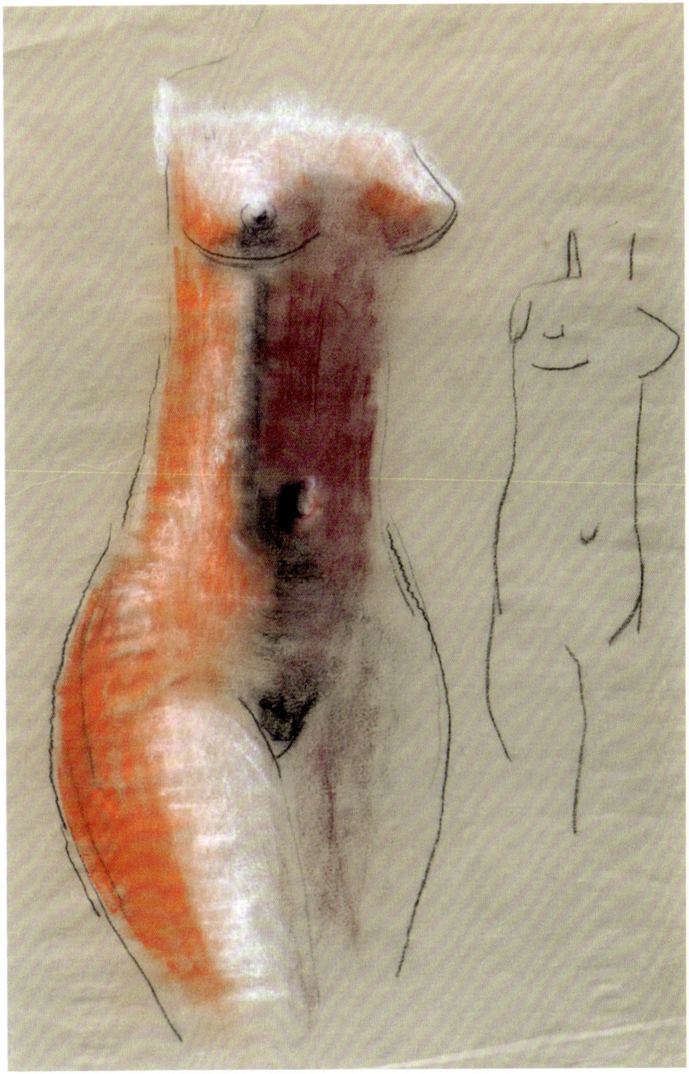

Romantic, watercolour & gouache, 1935, signed, 61.5 x 56.7 cm
Study of Standing Nude, chalk & charcoal, 51 x 35 cm

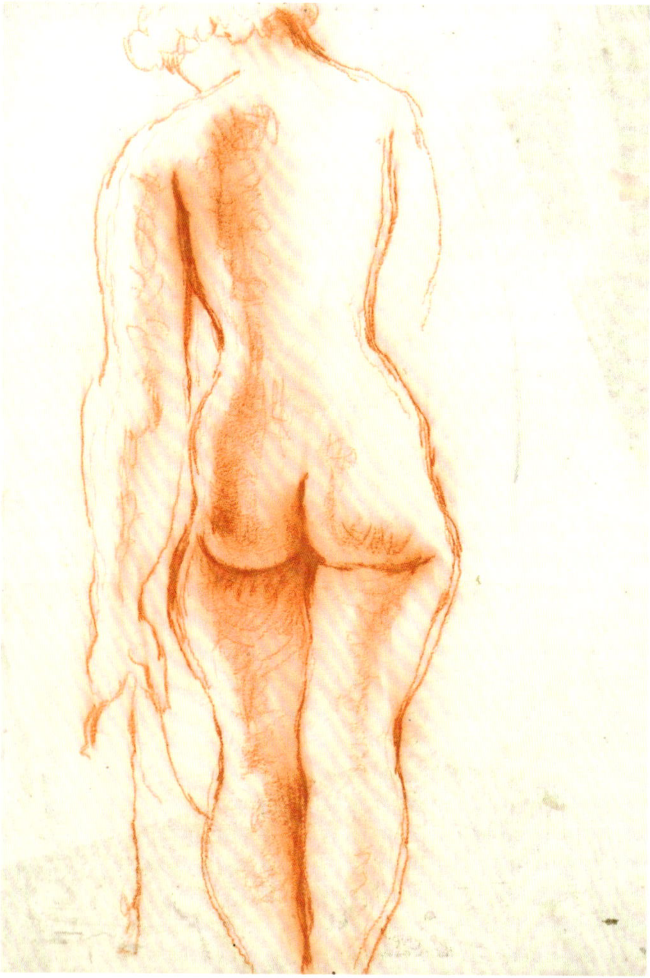

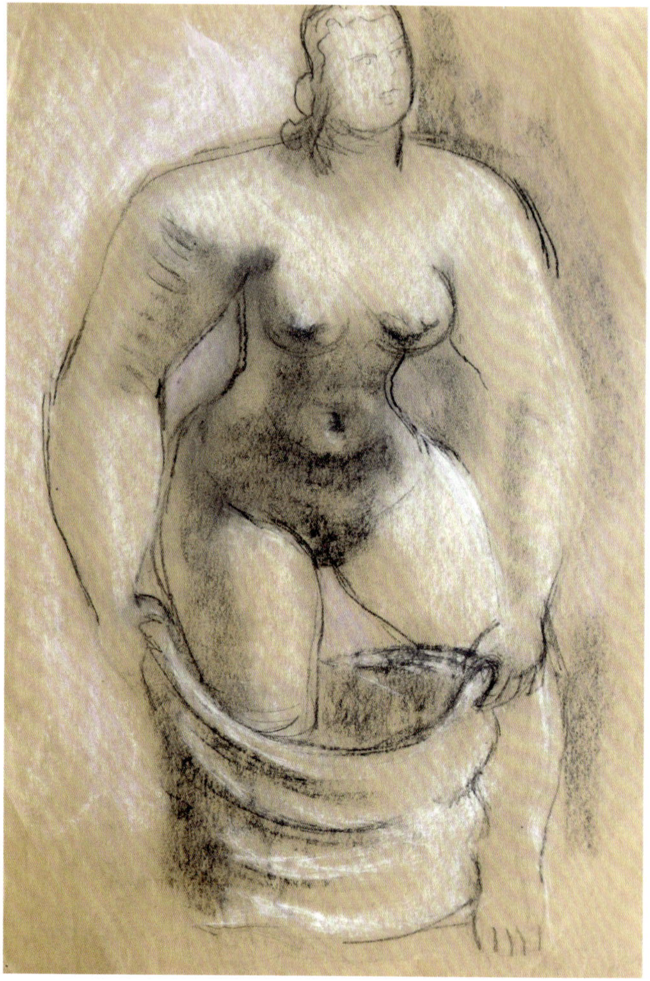

Terracotta Nude Facing Away, red chalk, estate stamp verso, 51 x 22 cm
Bather with Towel, chalk, 38 x 28 cm
Seated Figure, red chalk, 35.5 x 25.5 cm

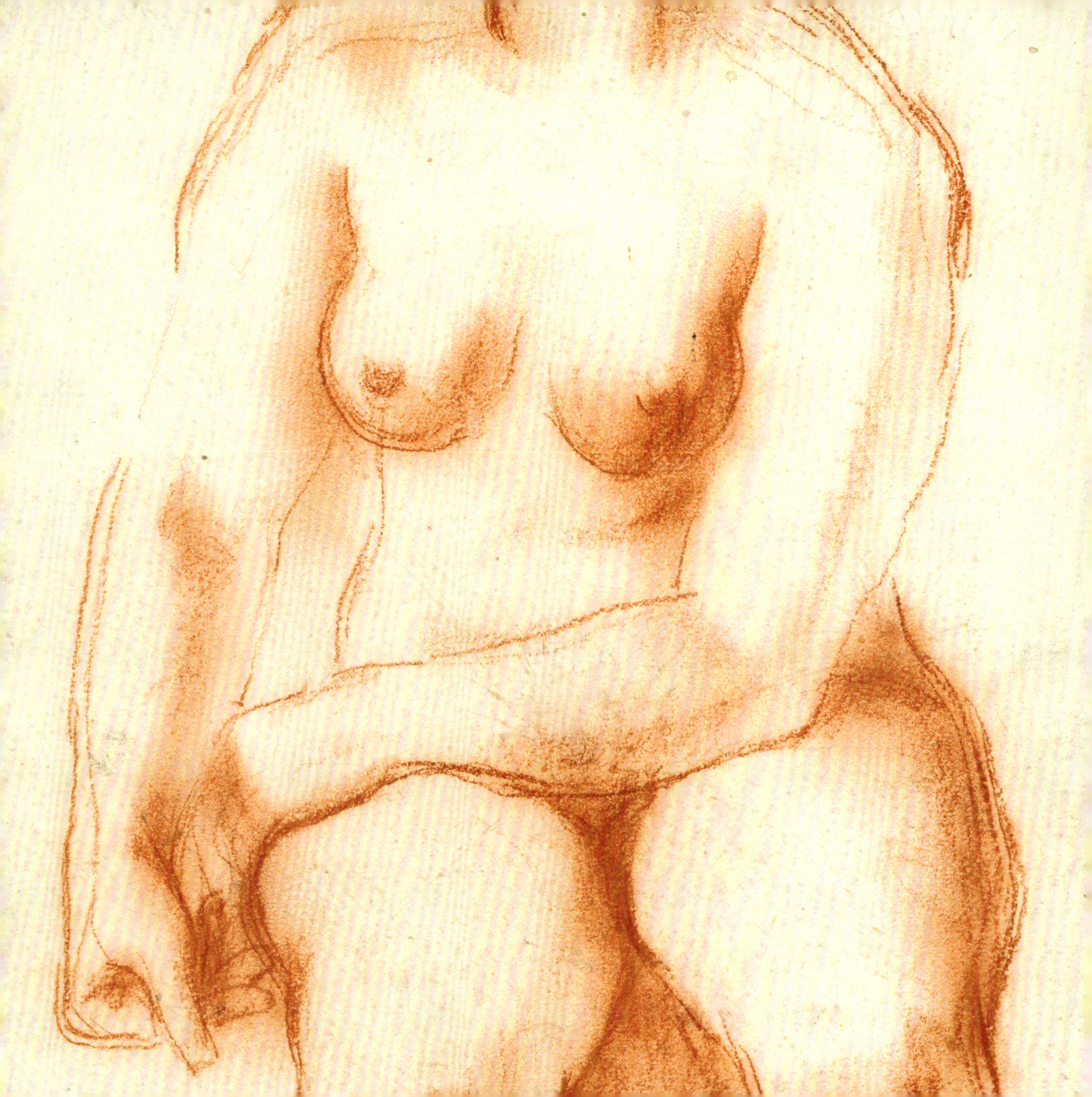

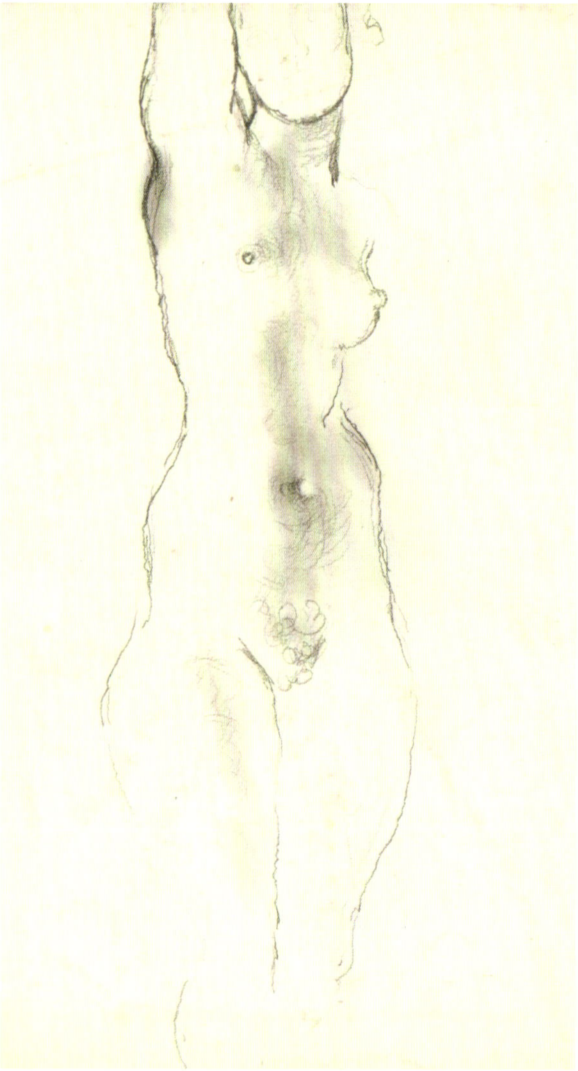

In 1942 Dobson had been elected an Associate of the Royal Academy (ARA), a junior category later abolished, but this was by no means an indicator of him joining the Establishment. It was essentially a financial move: he needed the RA's shop window to sell his work. He was not good with money and his financial affairs were often in disarray. In 1951 he was elected a full RA, and this combined with his job as Professor of Sculpture at the Royal College of Art (1946-53), led some critics to the easy but wrong-headed assumption that Dobson was now an academic. In fact he was a successful and thoughtful Professor, as he no doubt would have been when he was first proposed for the job in 1924. But back in the Twenties Sir William Rothenstein had pronounced him 'unsafe'. Perhaps he was too unacademic, even radical? (As Dobson said: 'Anything revolutionary was rather suspect, especially in this country.') Revealingly, it was Henry Moore who put Dobson forward for the position on both occasions, as if appointment to the RCA would somehow ensure Dobson was out of the running as a professional sculptor by turning him into a teacher who would no longer be poaching on what Moore increasingly saw as his exclusive preserves.

At the beginning of the 1950s Dobson started

Standing Nude IV, pencil, 51 x 15 cm
Study for Woman with a Bowl, bronze, 2020, ed 12, estate stamp, h 33 cm
Cast from the original 1952-3 plaster

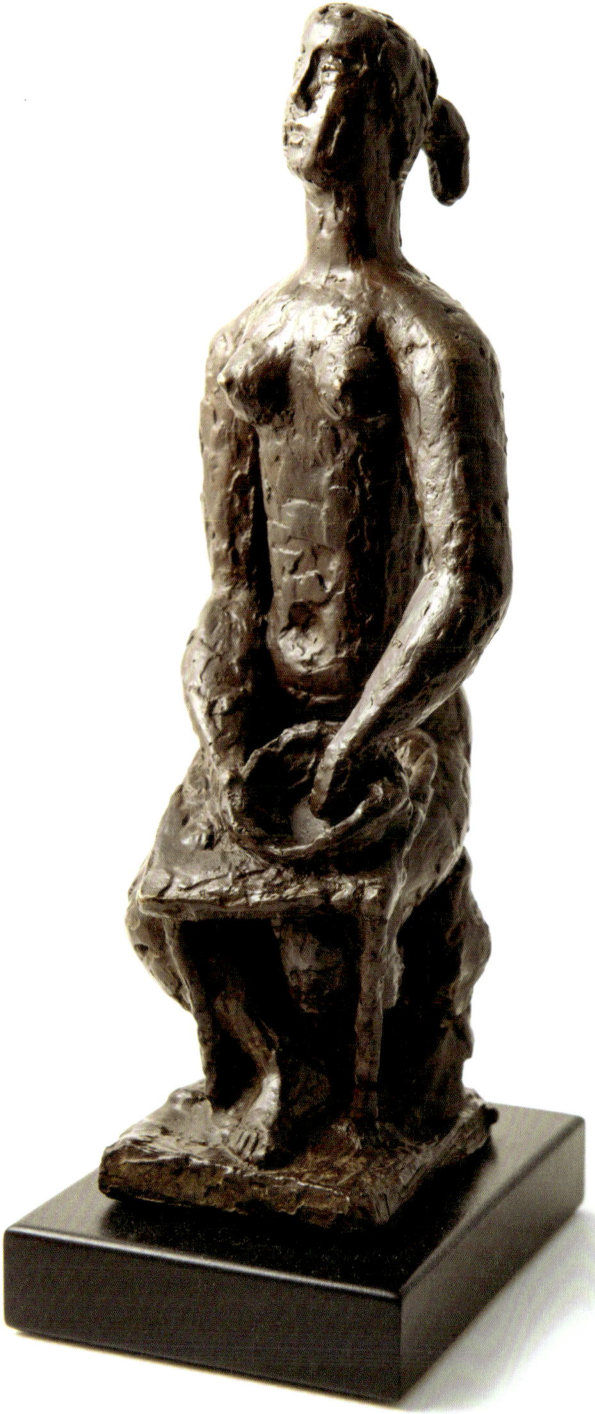

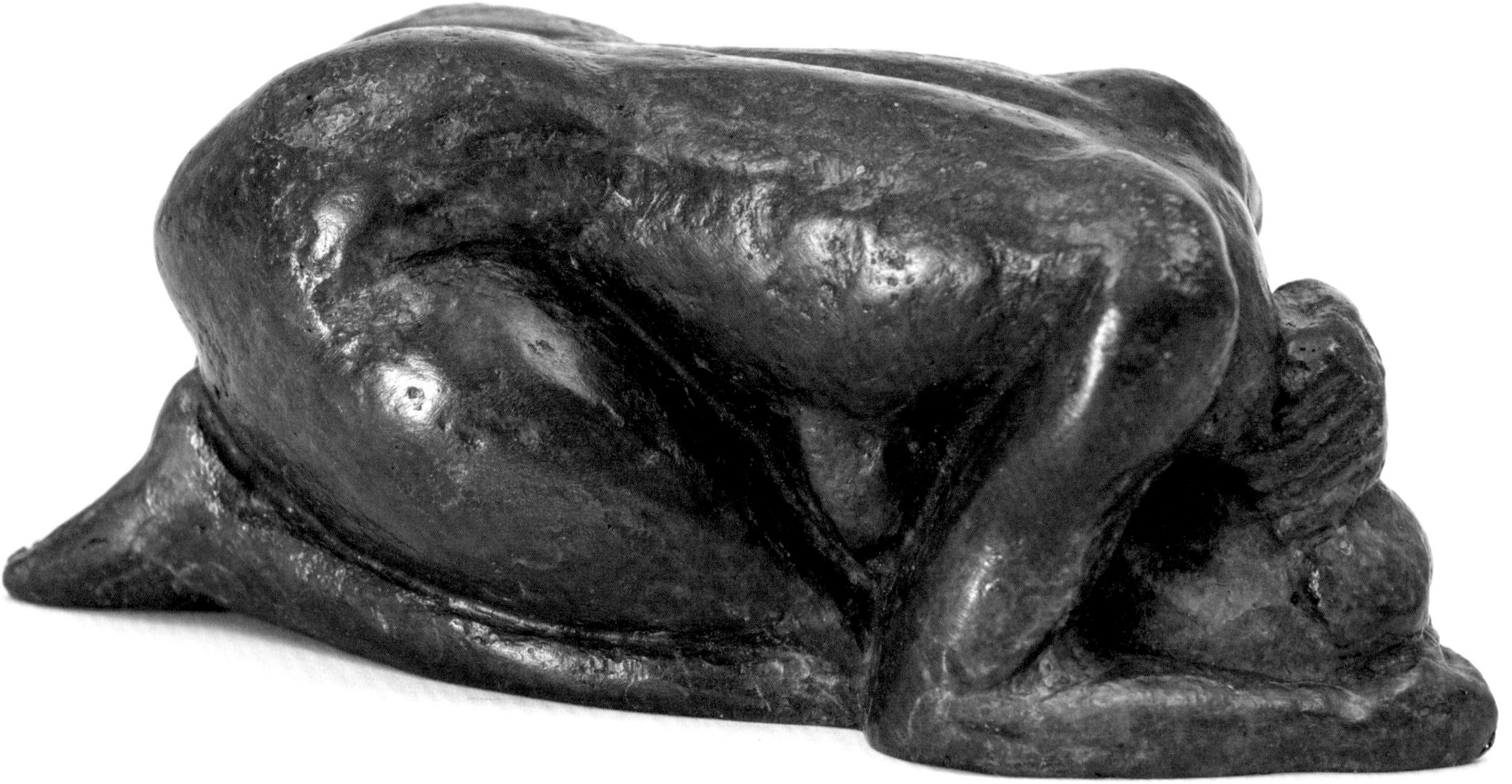

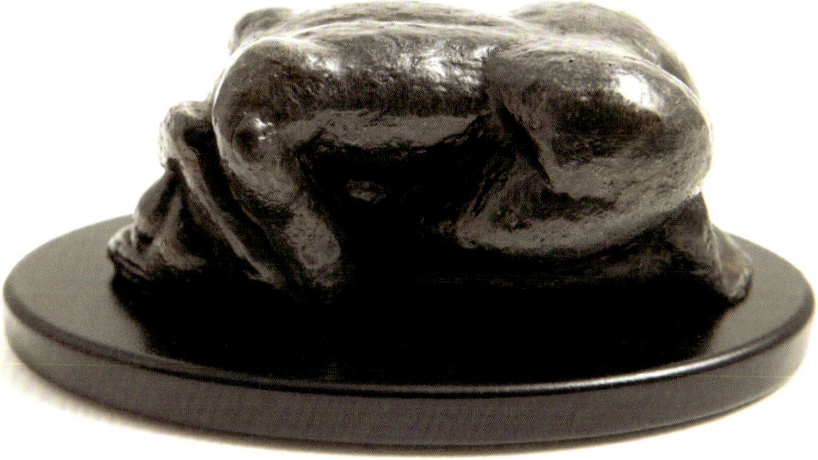

to write a series of autobiographical notes, but did not get very far. He returned to the project at the start of the next decade, dictating the material to his wife Mary. His memoirs eventually filled eight blue school exercise books, but only covered the early years of his life, up to the end of the 1920s. Perhaps it was no coincidence that the challenge of Moore and Hepworth to Dobson's ascendancy in the sculptural firmament began to make itself felt in the later 1920s and became fully manifest in the 1930s. Here began the eclipse of his achievement, in particular by Moore, that his work was to suffer posthumously, but Dobson hadn't the temperament to reassert himself. He was appealingly modest, as this remark makes plain: 'I always feel my own shows ought to look about five times as good as they do when I see them. It's an awful disease trying to make works of art.' Hard to imagine Moore saying that.

After the wartime destruction of the Manresa Road studio, and various stopgap addresses, Dobson moved to a much-loved house and studio in Harley Gardens, Kensington, and lived

left & above: **Crouching Nude**, bronze, 2020, ed 12, estate stamp, h 7.5 cm
Cast from the unique estate bronze. Not in the Catalogue Raisonné

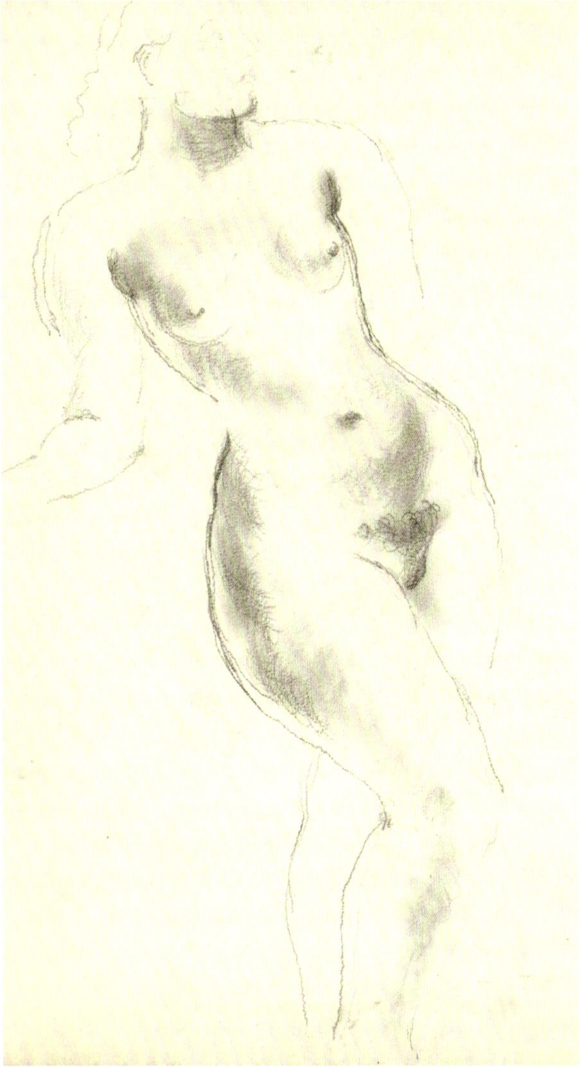

there until the lease unfortunately expired in January 1961 and he was forced to move again. He ended his days renting No 4 Stamford Bridge Studios in Fulham.

Brian Sewell (1931-2015), former art critic of the *Evening Standard*, and himself no great admirer of Dobson's work, was asked to help clear the Stamford Bridge studio after the sculptor's death in July 1963. He watched appalled and helpless as Mary Dobson destroyed anything she deemed erotic: tearing up and burning literally hundreds of chalk drawings and smashing clay and terracotta models. Although Sewell pleaded for these, recognising in them not only beauty but a life-affirming quality not always present in Dobson's later work, Mary was implacable. As Sewell observed, these studies of sexual congress were just as explicit as anything by Eric Gill, and he believed that Dobson's reputation suffered greatly from their annihilation.

Crawling Woman (c1944) is one of the more overtly erotic subjects which survived the cataclysm, as a unique terracotta. Now she is cast in bronze with a seductive silvery pewter patina and gold highlights. Notice her wasp waist and enhanced haunches and calves. *Europa and the Bull* (1946) — the other erotic sculpture among this group of works — takes as its subject

Leaning Nude, pencil, 51 x 25.5 cm
Europa and the Bull, bronze, 2021, ed 12, estate stamp, h 11.5 cm
Cast from the 1946 plaster

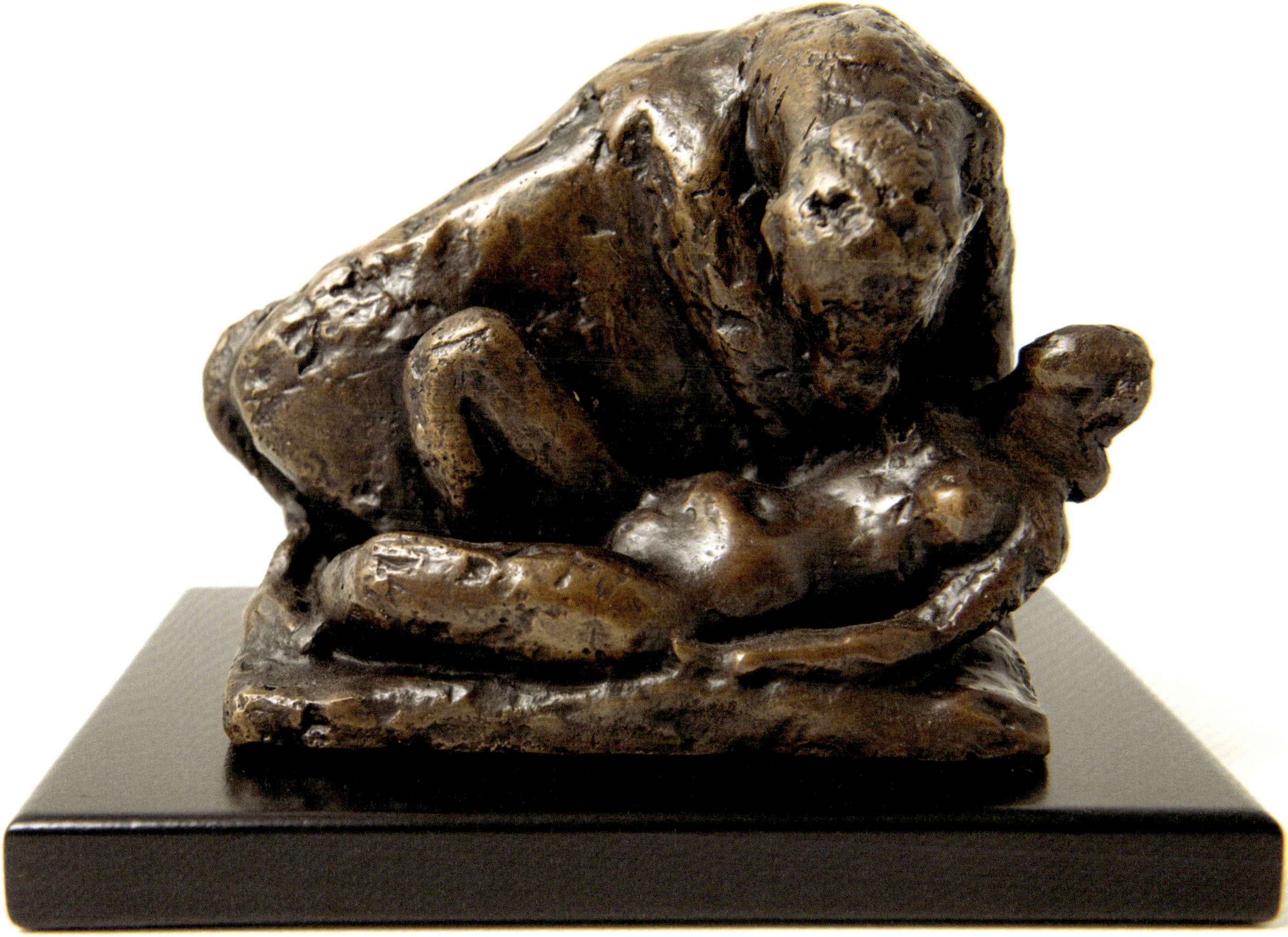

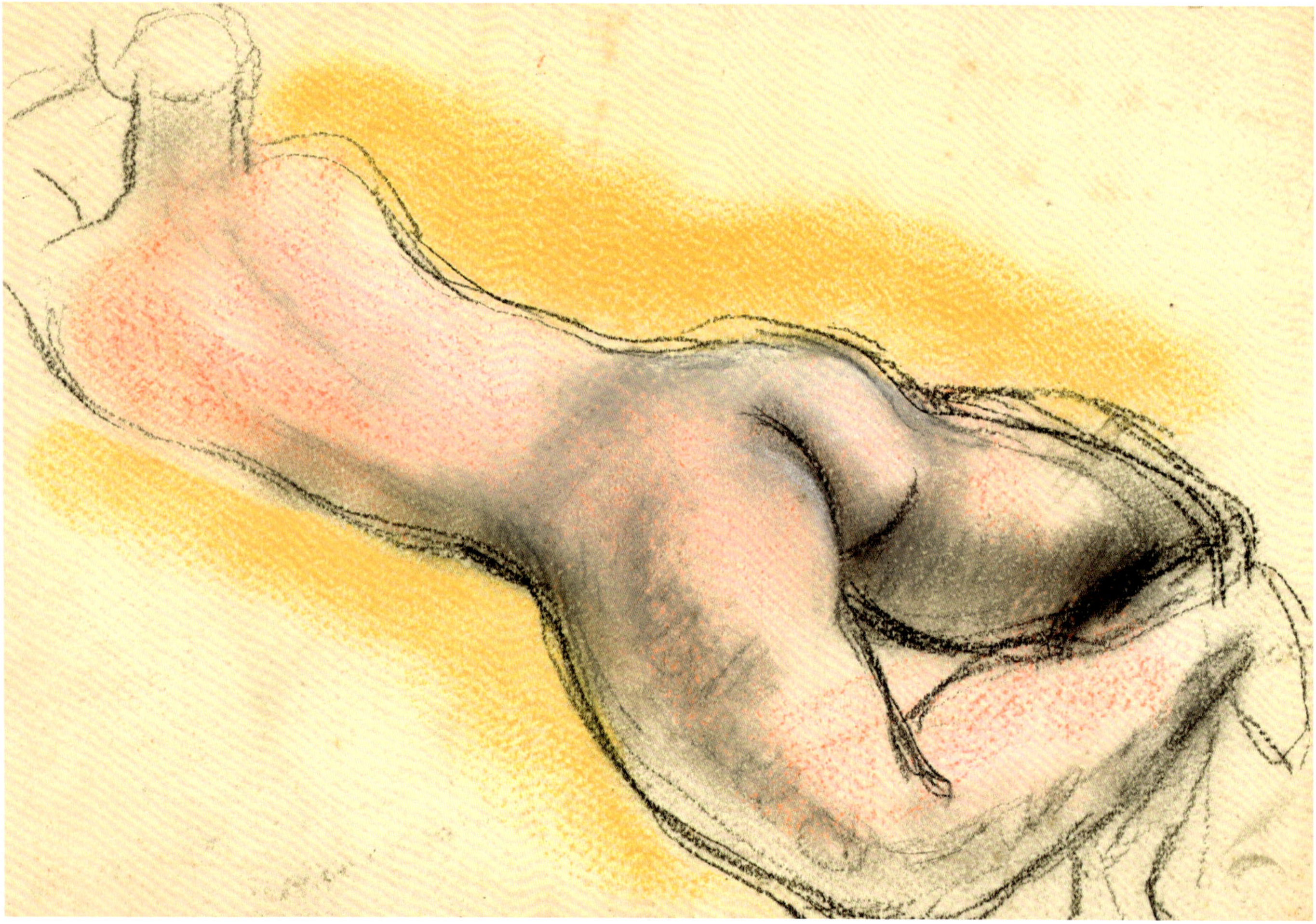

Nude Lying on Front, chalk, c.1940s, estate stamp verso, 17 x 25 cm
Crawling Woman, bronze, 2021, ed 12, estate stamp, h 15 cm
Cast from the 1944 terracotta

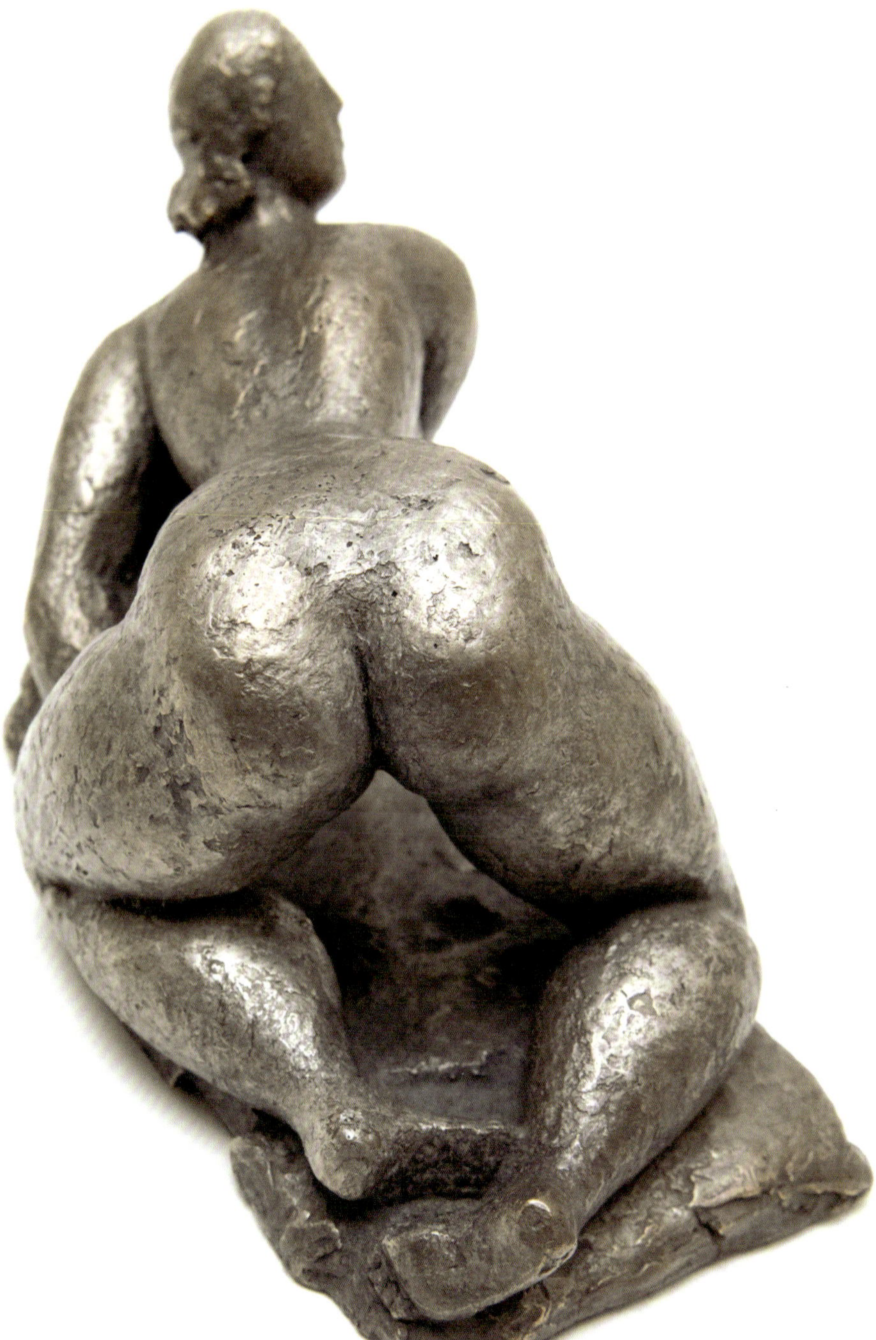

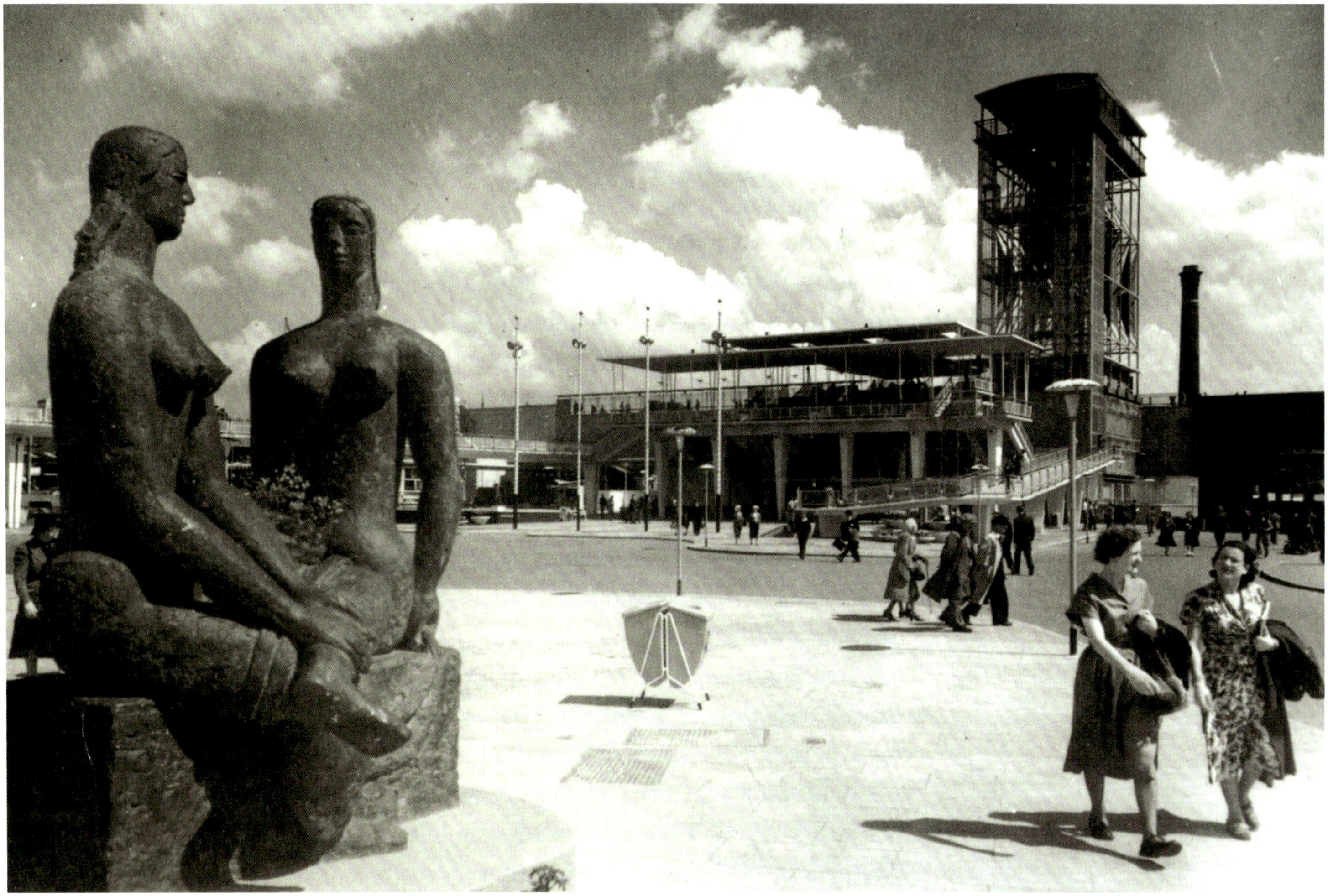

London Pride, The South Bank, Festival of Britain, 1951. Photographer unknown

the encounter of Zeus in the form of a bull, with the daughter of a legendary king of Tyre. The warm brown patina of this piece enhances the intimacy of the embrace, as the bull nuzzles Europa's left breast. But it's pretty mild stuff, and offers scant justification for holding it on a charge of impropriety as the American Customs did when it was sent over to the USA for exhibition.

Dobson had been working on a figure group on the theme of Leisure when he was commissioned by the Arts Council to make a large outdoors sculpture for the Festival of Britain. This was to be known as *London Pride (Leisure)*, probably his best-known public sculpture. *Study for London Pride (Leisure 3),* a terracotta from 1950 which had originally lost an arm, has now had her right arm restored and has been cast in bronze. It is of course a variation on one of Dobson's obsessions, two girls in silent colloquy, as already seen in *Noon* of 1935-6.

The water carrier, first modelled in the late 1920s or 1930, is another recurrent subject in Dobson's work and reappears in the 1940s as *Nude with a Pitcher* and *The Fount*. A related topic is *Woman and Fish*, for which there is a darkly emotive drawing, no doubt a study for the fountain sculptures Dobson made on this theme — a concrete one in Northampton, and a *ciment*

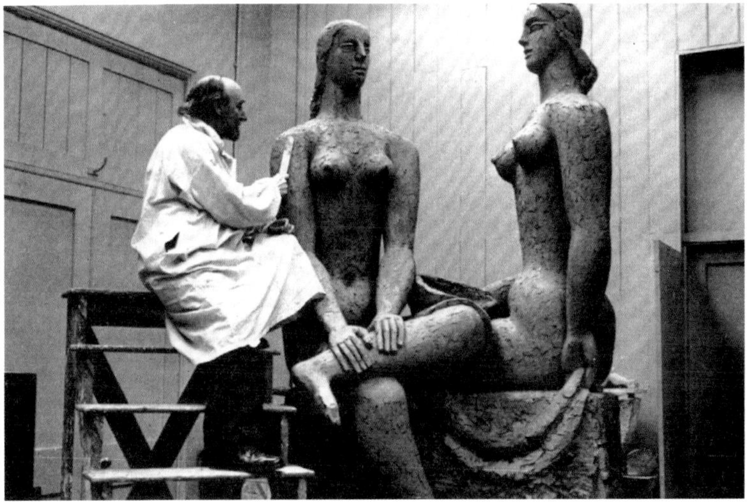

fondu one commissioned by London County Council for Tower Hamlets. These were produced in 1951, the year of the Festival of Britain, when *London Pride* was first displayed on the South Bank in its original plaster form, before being cast in bronze in 1987 and permanently sited there.

Despite age and infirmity, Dobson continued to experiment with form, changing the profile of his figures as and when his invention demanded. While none of his girls were ever as exiguous as Giacometti's, their robust outlines were from time to time slimmed down. Note the unexpectedly slender forms of *Study for Persephone 3* (1935),

Frank Dobson working on **London Pride**, 1950. Photographer unknown
next page: **Study for London Pride (Leisure 3)**, bronze, 2016, ed 9, estate stamp, h 28 cm
Cast from the 1950 terracotta

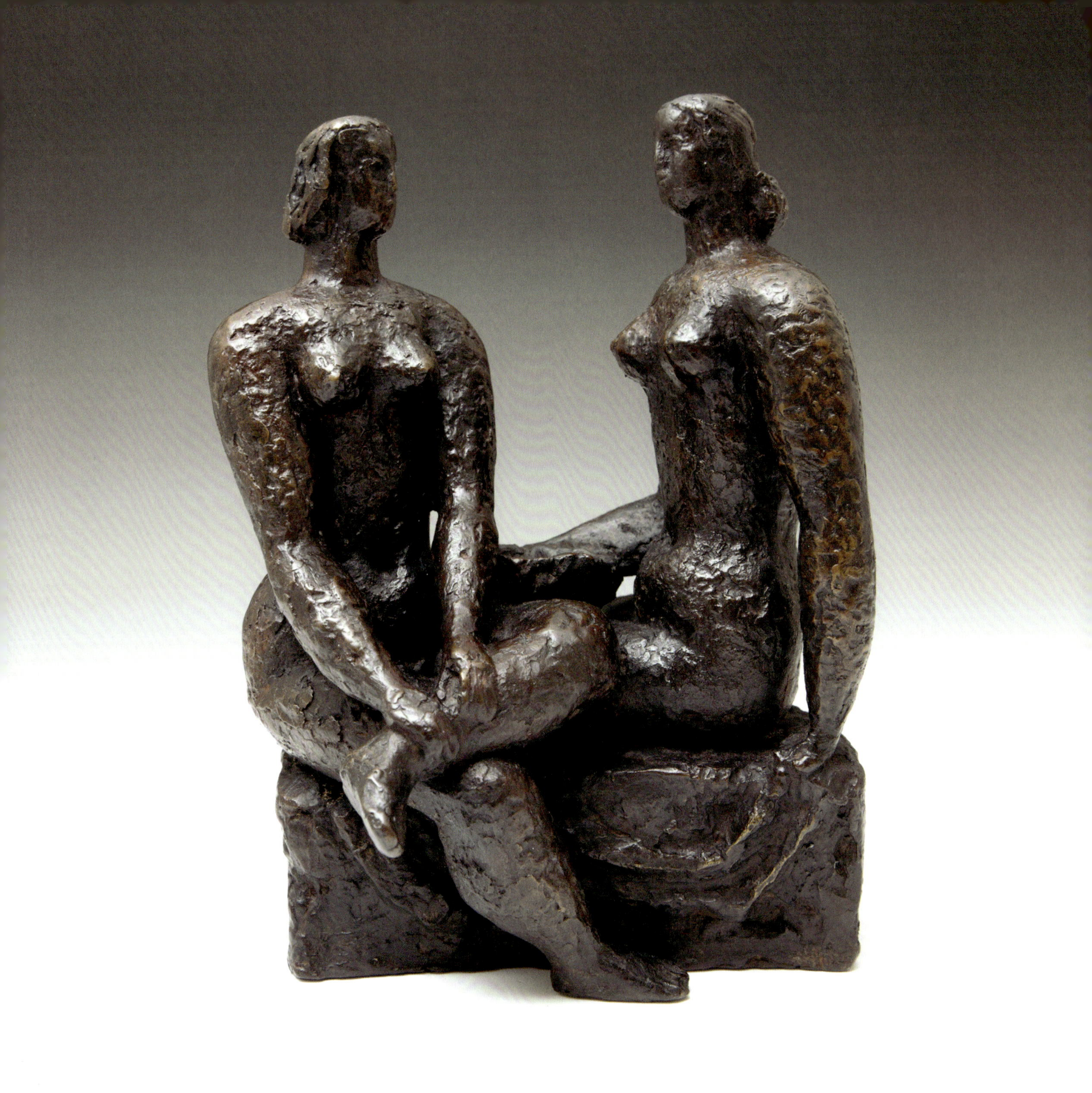

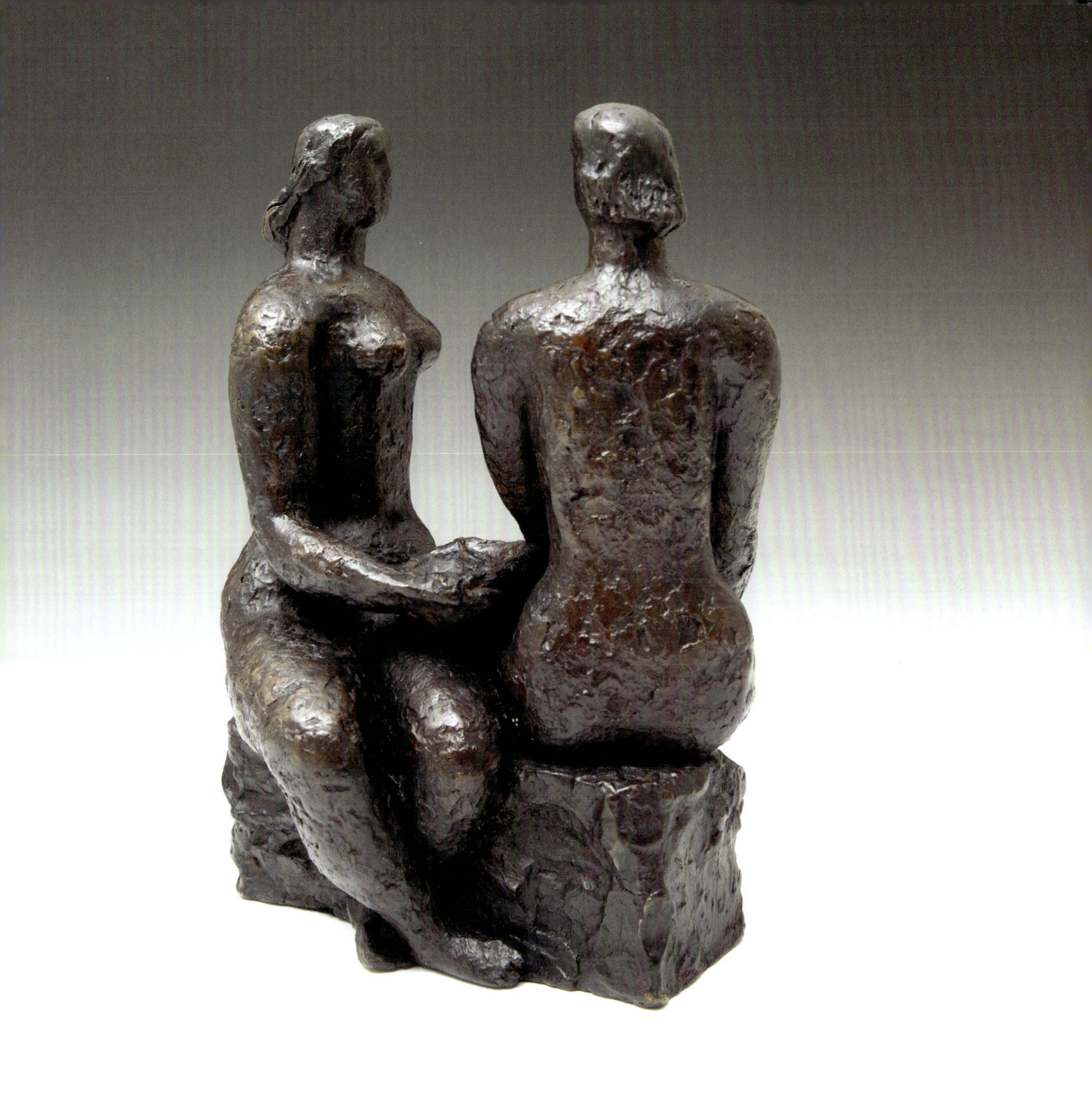

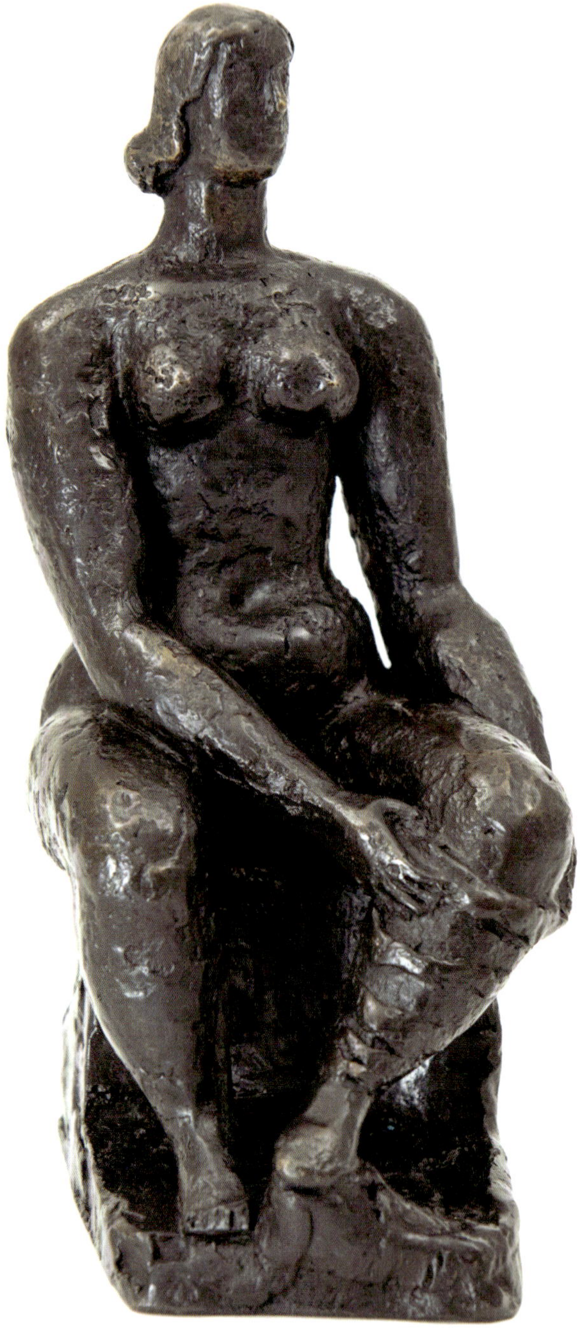

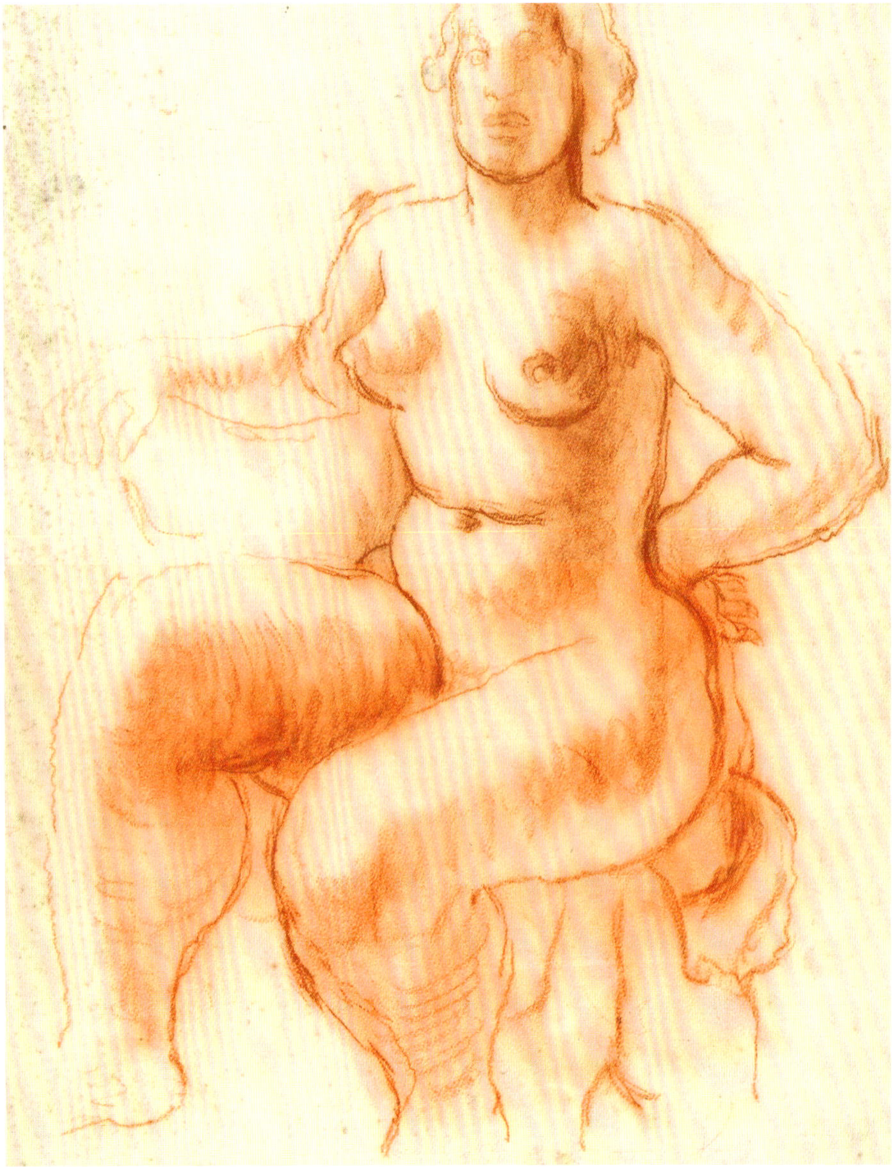

Study for Toilet 2, bronze, 2021, ed 12, estate stamp, h 17 cm
Cast from the 1939 terracotta
Study for Toilet, red chalk, 33 x 44 cm

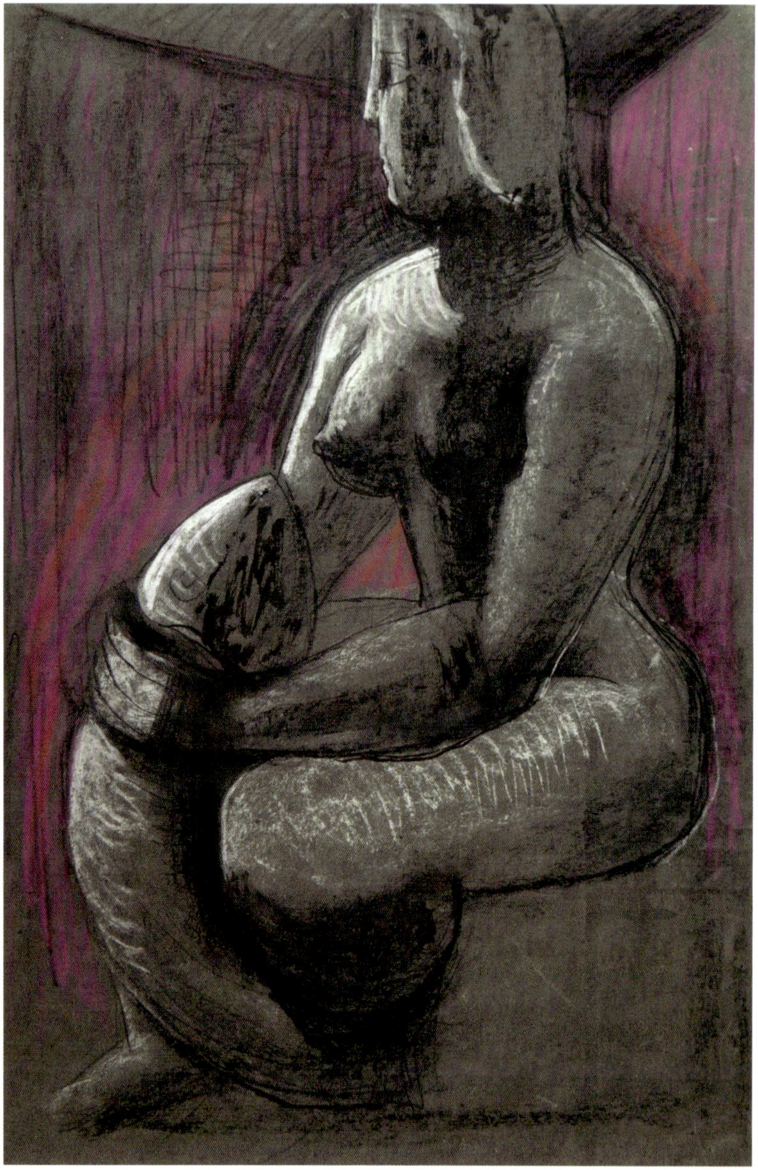

Woman with Fish II, chalk & ink, 55 x 37 cm
Seated Nude on a Chair, bronze, 2020, ed 12, estate stamp, h 20 cm
Cast from the 1940 plaster

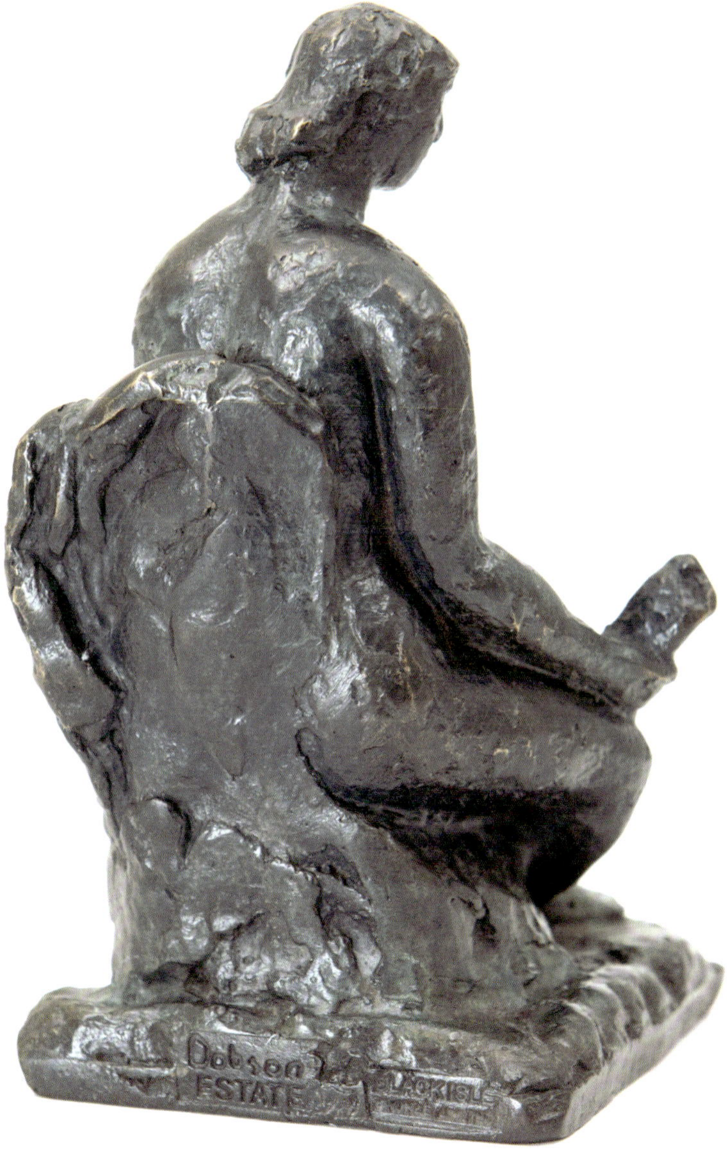
Dobson
ESTATE

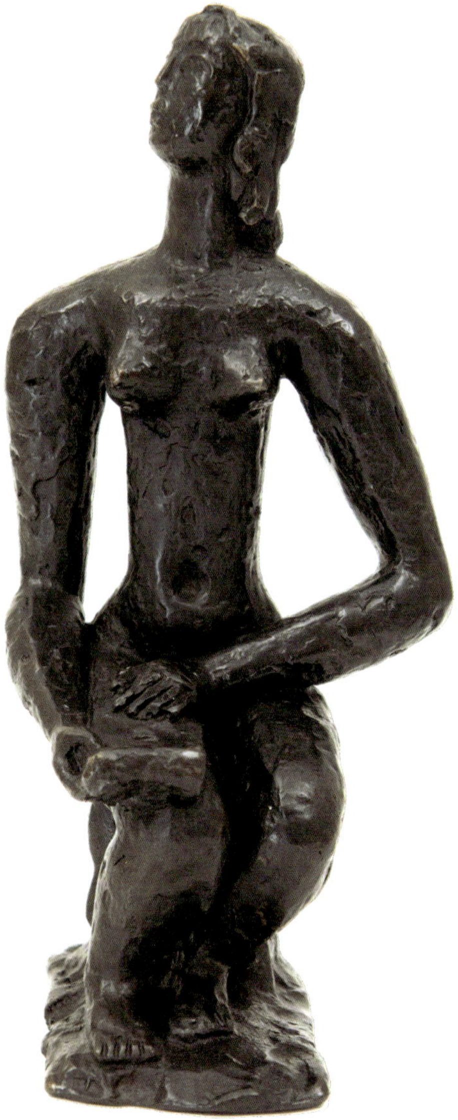

from the middle of his career, and *Woman with Scroll* (c1952-3) from the end. The latter began three-dimensional life as a unique hand-coloured plaster and has now been cast in bronze. It is strangely haunting, like a Recording Angel with a list of life's credits and debits, to which she is holding each of us accountable.

Reassuringly Dobson did not entirely relinquish his well-covered female forms, as another late sculpture, *Seated Leaning Figure* of 1953, clearly demonstrates. This unique terracotta, now superbly cast in bronze with golden shadows, delivers an unusual and slight uncomfortable-looking pose, to which the girl's body responds, bulging compensatingly. It's an odd and imaginative variation on Dobson's various sitting and leaning figures made over the years and reminds us that he continued to break new ground, even in his later period.

It's abundantly clear from this brief study of his sculptures and drawings that there are qualities of life and truth in Dobson's work arising from the directness of his response to attitudes of the body. His characteristic flowing curves may seem to be more about form than subject, but abstraction was never a real option for him. His primary inspiration remained the female figure. Whether worked in stone, plaster, terracotta or

Woman with Scroll, bronze, 2021, ed 12, estate stamp, h 23.5 cm
Cast from the unique 1952-3 plaster
Seated Leaning Figure, bronze, 2021, ed 12, estate stamp, h 25 cm
First cast from the unique 1953 terracotta

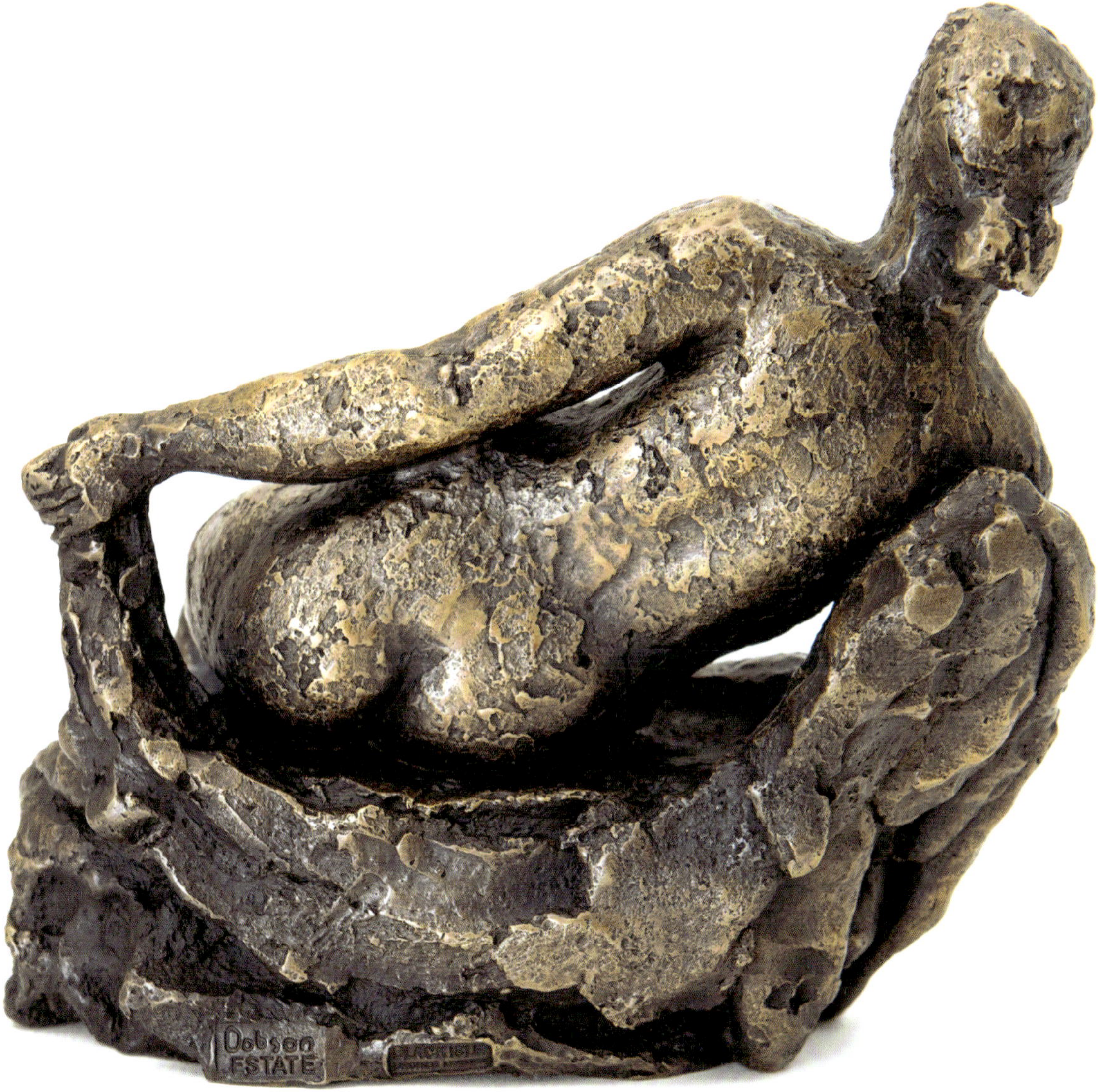
Dobson
ESTATE

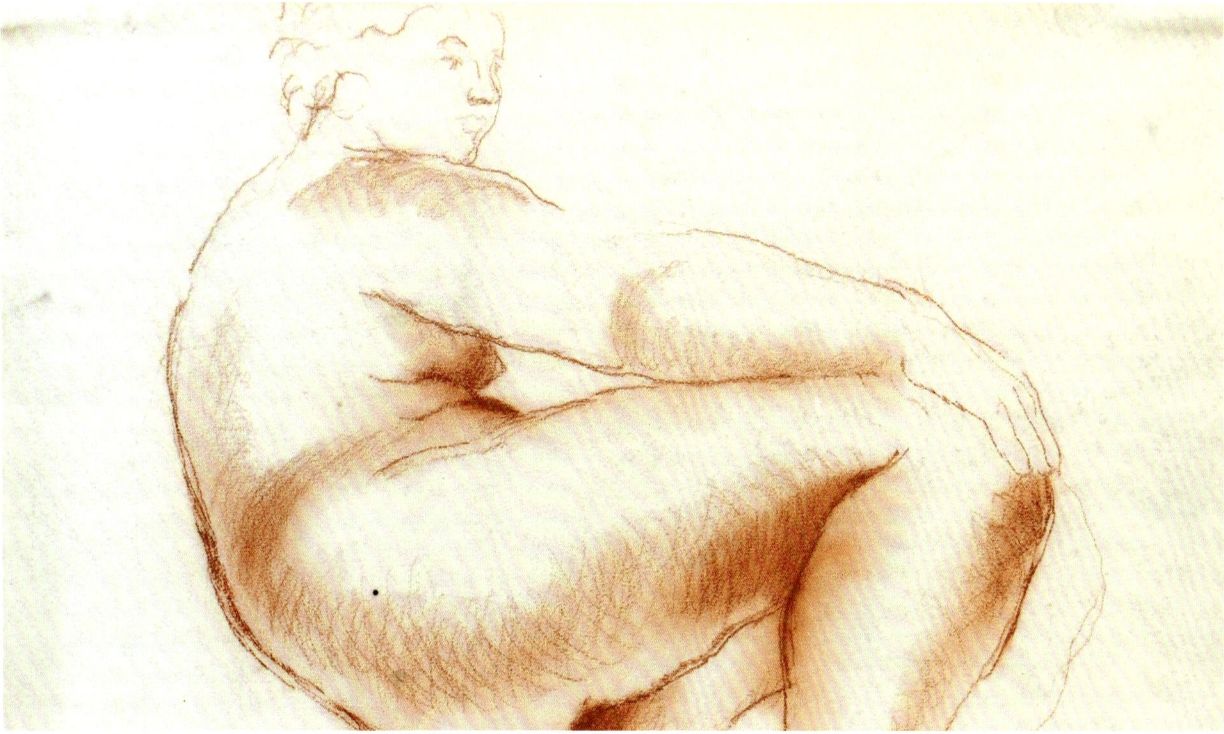

bronze, his figures have an architectural quality, but are also of the earth. Their apparent simplicity masks a formal complexity, but a complexity that has a beguiling naturalness to it. The mood is gentle and sensuous, but serious, and the best work possesses both grace and grandeur.

Dobson was probably at his finest when working closely with the model from direct observation. When he could translate his visual research into something beyond the real, capturing that essential quality of a thing or person, his work is dynamic and extremely exciting. The best of the drawings and the best of the sculptures achieve this, and this is what makes Frank Dobson's work so rewarding to look at and live with.

Woman Reclining, red chalk, 1940, signed, 23.5 x 50.7 cm